THE PSYCHOLOGY OF LEARNING

DR. YOGESHVER PRASAD SHARMA

ISBN 979-888569261-8

THE

PSYCHOLOGY

OF

LEARNING

Dr. Yogeshver Prasad Sharma

Associate Professor & Principal

School of Education

Shri Venkateshwara University, Gajraula (Amroha) UP, India

CONTENTS

PREFACE

1. PSYCHOLOGY OF LEARNING
2. METHODS OF STUDYING PSYCHOLOGY OF LEARNING
3. GROWTH AND DEVELOPMENT
4. LEARNING
5. LEARNING THEORIES
6. FACTORS AFFECTING LEARNING
7. MENTAL PROCESSES RELATED TO LEARNING
8. MEMORY
9. PERSONALITY
10. INTELLIGENCE
11. CREATIVITY
12. GROUP DYNAMICS

PREFACE

The psychology of learning is a theoretical science that covers the various psychological theories that relate to learning. Throughout history, there have been many various psychological learning theories. Some take on a more behaviorist approach which focuses on inputs and reinforcements.

Other approaches, such as theories related to neuroscience and social cognition, focus more on the brain's organization and structure to define learning. Some psychological approaches, such as social constructivism, focus more on one's interaction with the environment and with others. Other theories, such as those related to motivation, like the growth mindset, focus more on the individual.

The psychology of learning is also very applicable today. There has been extensive research in recent years that looks closely at how students are learning both inside and outside the classroom. This information is used to present new and more cooperative approaches to homework, tests, and the student's ability to learn. Theories related to the psychology of learning can also help to explain and improve student performance, motivation, and investment in their learning.

It is hoped that this book would meet the requirements of not only the students of education but also all those who are interested in the psychology of learning.

Any suggestions for the improvement of this book will be gratefully accepted.

Dr. Yogeshver Prasad Sharma

CHAPTER-1

PSYCHOLOGY OF LEARNING

Unit Structure:

0. Objective
1. Introduction
2. Meaning and Definition of Educational psychology
3. Nature Of Educational Psychology
4. Scope of Educational Psychology

0. OBJECTIVE

After going through this unit carefully you should be able to

- Define Educational Psychology.
- Explain the nature of Educational Psychology.
- List out the functions of Educational Psychology.

1. INTRODUCTION

This is the first unit of the second paper of Psychology of Learning. This course deals with the importance and contribution of educational psychology on the theory and practice of education. every teacher is confronted with the problem of individuals difference in the classroom. The purpose of this unit is to define the concept of educational Psychology. It describes meaning and nature of Educational Psychology. An attempt has also been made to describe the characteristics and meaning of learning.

1. MEANING AND DEFINITION OF EDUCATIONAL PSYCHOLOGY

Educational Psychology and consists of two words Psychology and Education. While General Psychology is a pure science. Educational Psychology is its application in the field of education with the aim of socializing man and modifying his behavior. According to Crow and Crow Educational Psychology describes and explains the learning experiences of an individual from birth through old age. Skinner defines Educational Psychology as "that branch of Psychology which deals with teaching and learning"

Stephen – "Educational Psychology is the systematic study of the educational growth and development of a child."

Judd – "Educational Psychology is the Science which explains the changes that take place in the individuals as they pass through the various stages of development." Peel- "Educational Psychology is the science of Education."

Educational psychology is one of the branches of applies psychology concerned with the application of the principles, techniques and other resource of psychology to the solution of the problems confronting the teacher attempting to direct the growth of children toward defined objectives. More specifically, we can say educational psychology is concerned with an understanding of:

- The child, his development, his need and his potentialities.
- The learning situation including group dynamics as the affect learning.
- The learning processes its nature and the ways to make it effective. Stated differently, the Central theme of Educational Psychology is Psychology of learning.

PSYCHOLOGY OF LEARNING

This area is concerned with such problems as : How do children acquire skills? When is learning more effective? What are the factors that help the learning Process? How do we measure the amount of learning? Are there any economic methods of memorizing? Why do we forget? Can memory be improved? Dose the study of Sanskrit helps than study of Hindi?

Psychology helps the teacher to get answers to these questions. It tells us that learning becomes more effective if factors like motivation and interest are taken into consideration by every teacher. The knowledge of psychology has helped the teacher in modifying her approach to the teaching learning process.

The study of educational Psychology has brought about change in the approach and therefore we have child centered education. Psychological principles are used in formulation curriculum for different stage. Attempts are made to provide subjects and activities in the curriculum which are in conformity with the needs of the students, their developmental characteristics, learning patterns and also needs of the society.

3. NATURE OF EDUCATIONAL PSYCHOLOGY

Following are the important characteristics of the nature of educational psychology:

- It is an applied branch of fundamental Psychology.
- It combines two fields i.e. education and psychology.
- It is the scientific study of human behavior in educational situation.
- It is concerned with these factors, principles and techniques which relate to the various aspects of child's growth and development.
- It is concerned with learning situation and process by which learning can be more efficient and effective.
- Educational Psychology, draws heavily from various branches of psychology, biology sociology and anthropology
- Educational Psychology is not as exact as natural sciences since the human behavior cannot be predicated exactly, because it is dynamic.
- Educational Psychology is a science of education dealing primarily with how, when and what of education.

- It is not a normative a science as it is not concerned with the value of educational and doesn't concern itself with and 'What ought to be." It only describes what it is; it is an applied positive science.
- While psychology deals with the behavior of all individuals in all walks of life. Educational Psychology limits its dealing with the behavior of the pupil in relation to Educational environment.
- It does not concern with what and why of education it gives the necessary knowledge and skill (Technical Guidance) for giving education the pupil in a satisfactory way.

SCOPE OF EDUCATIONAL PSYCHOLOGY

Evaluation of Learning outcome

Teaching Strategies

Learning content (curriculum)

Learning Process

Teacher

Leaner

4. SCOPE OF EDUCATIONAL PSYCHOLOGY

Five major areas covered by Educational Psychology are:

- The Learner
- The learning Process
- The learning Situation
- The Teaching Situation
- Evaluation of Learning Performance
- The Teacher

The Learner

Educational Psychology acquaints us with need of knowing the leaves and deals with the techniques of knowing him well. Following are the topics studied included in it: the innate abilities and capabilities of the individual differences and their measurements, the overt, convert, conscious as well as unconscious behavior of the learner, the characteristics of his growth and development at each stage beginning from childhood to adulthood.

The Learning Process

After knowing the learner and deciding what learning experiences are to be provided, the emerging problem is to help learner in acquiring these learning experiences with ease and confidence.

Hence, it deals with the nature of learning and how it take place and contains the topics such as laws, principles and theories of learning;

remembering and forgetting, perceiving, concept formation, thinking, reasoning process, problem solving, transfer of training, ways and means of effective learning etc.

Learning Situation

It also deals with the environment factors and learning situation which come midway between the learner and the teacher. Topics like classroom climate and group dynamics techniques and aids which facilitate learning, evaluation techniques, and practices, guidance and counseling etc. which help in the smooth functioning of the teaching learning process.

Teaching Situation

It suggests the techniques of teaching. It also helps in deciding what learning situation should be provided by teacher to learner according to his mental and physical age, his previous knowledge and interest level. By describing the learner's characteristics, what teaching aids are appropriate for the particular subject?

Evaluation of Learning Performance

Main objective of education is all-round development of the learner. It includes cognitive, affective and psychomotor aspects of personality. Educational Psychology suggests various tool and techniques for assessment and evaluation such as performance test, oral test and written test. It does not stop at measurement only, after the testing results of the test are analyzed causes for poor performance, backwardness in any aspect of development is corrected by maladjustment are helped by guidance and counselling study habit, examination techniques and learning styles are analyzed and helped the learner so that he can overcome the difficulties.

The Teacher

Educational Psychology emphasizes the need of knowing the self for a teacher to play his role properly in the process of education. It throws light on the essential personality traits, interests, aptitudes, the characteristics of effective teaching etc., so as to inspire, help teacher handle the stress, conflict and anxiety by giving insight in their own personality.

Unit End Exercises:

1. Knowledge of Educational Psychology helps teacher in ....

A. Obtaining the B.Ed. degree

B. It is ethical to have the knowledge of Educational Psychology.
C. Improving the socio-emotional climate of the class.
D. Teaching the special type of children.

2. Educational Psychology aims to ......

A. To decide the future of the learner
B. To forecast the future behavior of the learner.
C. Improve learning situation by descending learning's needs and interest.
D. To control the Educational Programme.

????

CHAPTER-2

METHODS OF STUDYING PSYCHOLOGY OF LEARNING

A] INTROSPECTION B] OBSERVATION

C] EXPREMINENTAL

Unit Structure:

0. Objectives
1. Introduction
2. Introspection Method
3. Observation Method
4. Experimental Method

0. OBJECTIVES

After reading this unit, you will be able to:

- Describe the Introspection method
- State the merits and demerits on Introspection method
- Describe the observation method
- State the merits and demerits of observation method
- Explain the steps and demerits of observation method
- Explain the steps of experimental method
- State the merits and demerits of experimental method
- Describe the clinical method
- State the merits and demerits of clinical method

1. INTRODUCTION

Dear students in the preceding section, you have analyzed the nature, definition, scope and function of psychology of learning. We have also discussed the psychological concept of leering.

In this unit, we will describe the important methods of studying psychology of learning. Students all the method to study psychology of learning are basically methods of general psychology.

A brief review of the development of methods will be helpful for you to understand the important of the subject in greater perspective.

The first effort of conducting systematic experimental studies in psychology was stared in 1879 in Germany with the establishment of first laboratory of psychology by William Wundt.

The next important method of collecting data was evolved with the development of psychoanalysis an independent system of psychology by Sigmund Freud who emphasized importance of unconscious in understanding the behavior. In the second decade of 20th century, psychology developed as an objective science of behavior by the efforts of Pavlov Watson and Guthrie. Experimental and observation methods were developed to collect data to study behavior. Simultaneously testing movement started with the introduction of statistics in psychology.

Students here we will study only the following methods of studying psychology of learning. They are:

A. Introspection method B] Observation method C] Experimental method

2. INTROSPECTION METHOD

Students at many times, when you have experienced an emotion like anger or fear you begin to think reasons for the state of yours.

You say, "Why have I been annoyed over this or that? Why been afraid of such things" The analysis of your emotional state may take place simultaneously with the emotion or it may be done after the emotional state is over. In whatever manner it is done, it gives you an understanding, though rudimentary of your mind. This method of probing into your mental processes is a method of introduction utilized by psychologists in a much-refined manner.

Let us see in detail what do we mean by Introduction and its merits and demerits.

What we mean by introspection

Introduction is a method of self-observation. The word 'Introspection is made up of two Latin words. "Intro" meaning within and "Aspection" meaning looking. Hence it is a method where an individual is looking within one self.

Angel considered it as "looking inward". In Introduction the individual peeps into his own mental state and observes his own mental processes.

Stout considers that 'to introspect is to attend to the working of one's own mind in a systematic way'.

Introspection method is one of the oldest methods to collect data about the conscious experiences of the subject. It is a process of self – examination where one perceives, analyses and reports one's own feelings. Let us learn this process with the help of an example, suppose you are happy and in the state of happiness you look within yourself. It is said you are introspecting your own mental feelings and examining what is going on in your mental process in the state of happiness. Similarly, you may introspect in state of anger or fear; etc Introspection is also defined as the notice, which the mind takes of itself.

Let us see the stages distinguished in introspection. Students there are three clear stages in introspection.

1. During the observation of external object, the person beings to ponder over his own mental states. For example While listening to the music, which is to him pleasant or unpleasant he starts thinking about his own mental state.
2. The person begins to question the working of the his own mind. He thinks and analyses: Why has he said such and such thing? Why as he talked in a particular manner? And so on.
3. he tries to frame the laws and conditions of mental processes: He thinks in terms of improvement of his reasoning or the control of his emotional stages. This stage of that of the scientific methods for the advancement of our scientific knowledge.

Characteristics of Introspection:

Introspection being self- observation has the following characteristics:

1. The subject gets direct, immediate and intuitive knowledge about the mind.
2. The subject has actually to observe his own mental processes. He cannot speculate about them.

Students, Introduction Method was widely used in the past. Its use in modern time is being questioned. It is considered unscientific and not in keeping with psychology which has recently

emerged out as a positive science however we may say that it is still being used by psychologists and though its supremacy is undetermined, yet it is not totally discarded.

Merits of Introspection Method:

- It is the cheapest and most economical method. We do not need any apparatus or laboratory for its use.
- This method can be used anytime and anywhere you can introspect while walking, traveling, sitting on a bed & so on.
- It is the easiest method and is readily available to the individual.
- The introspection data are first hand as the person himself examines his own activities.
- Introspection has generated research which gradually led to the development of more objective methods.
- It is still used in all experimental investigation.
- It is the only method with the help of which and individual can know his emotions and feelings.

William James has pointed out the importance of this method in these words. "Introspective observation is what we have to rely on first and foremost and always. The word introspection can hardly be defined-it means, of course, looking into our own minds and reporting what we there discover. Everyone agrees that we there discover states of consciousness. So far as I know, the existence of such states has never been doubled by my critic, however skeptical in other respects we may have been."

Limitations of Introspection Methods:

- In introspection, one needs to observe or examine one's mental processes carefully in the form of thoughts, feeling and sensation. The state of one's mental processes is continuously changing therefore when one concentrates on introspecting a particular phase of one's mental activity that phases passes off. For example when you get angry at something and afterwards sit down to introspect calmly the state of anger is sure to have passed off and so what you try to observe is not what is happening at that time with yourself but what had happened sometime before.
- The data collected by introspection cannot be verified. An individual may not pass through the same mental state again. There is no independent way of checking the data.
- The data collected by introspection lacks validity and reliability. It is impossible to acquire validity and exactness in self-observation of one's own mental processes.

- The data collected by introspection in highly subjective. It has danger of being biased and influenced by preconceptions of the individual.
- The observer and the observed are the same. Hence there is ample scope for the individual to lie deliberately and hide the facts to mislead.
- Introspection cannot be applied to children, animal and abnormal people. It requires highly trained and skilled workers to introspect.
- Introspection us logically defective because one and the same person is the experiencer and observer. It is not possible for the

same individual to act as an experience as well as an observer.

There introspection is logically defective.

Conclusion:

The limitations of introspection can be overcome by practice and training, by remaining alters during introspection and by comparing results obtained by experts.

Check Your Progress:

Note a] Write your answers in the space given below.

b] Compare your answers with those given at the end of the unit.

1. Fill in the blanks:

A. Introspection is a method of -------------
B. The word introspection is made up of two Latin words ---------

- and

3. OBSERVATION METHOD

Student we observe so many things in nature. We also observe the action and behavior of others and form our own notions about this person. We look at other persons, listen to their talks and try to infer what they mean. We try to infer the characteristics, motivations, feelings and intentions of others on the basis of these observations. So let us study about Observation method employed by psychologists in detail.

With the development of psychology as an objective science of learning behavior, the method of introspection was replaced by careful observation of human and animal behavior to collect data by research workers.

In introspection we can observe the mental process of ourselves only, but in observation, we observe the mental processes of others. Hence Observation is the most commonly used for the study of human behavior.

Meaning of Observation

Observation literally means looking outside oneself. Facts are collected by observing overt behavior of the individual in order to locate underlying problem and to study developmental trends of different types.

The overt behavior is the manifestation of court conditions within the individual. The study of overt behavior gives indirectly the clue to the mental condition of the individual. Observation means 'perceiving the behavior as it is"

In the words of Goods, "Observation deals with the overt behavior of persons in appropriate situations."

Observation has been defined as "Measurements without instruments."

For example students in classroom have been labeled as good, fair or poor in achievement and lazy or diligent in study etc. on the basis of observation, observation is indirect approach to study the mental processes of others through observing their external behavior. For example if someone frowns, howls, grinds his teeth, closes his fists, you would say that the person is angry by only observing these external signs of his behavior.

Students in the process of observation, following four steps are generally required:

1. Observation of behavior:

The first step involved in the method of observation is directly perceiving or observing the behavior of individuals under study. For example, if we want to observe the social behavior of children we can observe it when they assemble and play.

2. Recording the behavior observed:

The observation should be carefully and immediately noted and recorded. Minimum time should be allowed to pass between happening and recording. It will make the observation more objective.

3. Analysis and Interpretation of behavior:

When the notes of behavior observed are completed, they are analyzed objectively and scientifically in order to interpret the behavior patterns.

4. Generalization:

On the basis of analysis and interpretation of the data collected with the help of observation method, it is possible to make certain generalization. Social –development and behavior of children have been described by child Psychologists on the basis of generalization based upon analysis and interpretation of the data gathered through the observation method.

Types of Observation:

Students you have just seen what observation is and how it is conducted.

Do you know there are different ways in which observation can be done, so let us see the different types of observation?

1. <u>Natural Observation:</u>

In natural observation we observe the specific behavioral characteristics of children in natural setting. Subject does not become conscious of the fact that their behavior is being observed by someone.

2. <u>Participant – Observation:</u>

Here the observer becomes the part of the group, which he wants to observe. It discloses the minute and hidden facts.

3. <u>Non-Participant Observation:</u>

Here the observer observes in such a position, which is least disturbing to the subject under study, the specific behavior is observed in natural setting without subject's getting conscious that they are observed by someone. Non-participant observation permits the use of recording instruments.

4. <u>Structure Observation:</u>

Here the observer in relevance sets up a form and categories in terms of which he wishes to analyze the problem. The observer always keeps in view

a] A frame of reference b] Time units.

c] Limits of an act

5. <u>Unstructured Observation:</u>

This is also called as uncontrolled or free observation. It is mainly associated with participant observation in which the observer assumes the role of a member of the group to be observed. Here the individual is observed when he is in his class, playground or when he is moving about with his friends and class follows without knowing that he is being observed.

Observation is very useful method to study child and his behavior. Student's observation method, being commonly used method psychology has following merits:

Merits of Observation Method

1. Being a record of actual behavior of the child, it is more reliable and objective.
2. It is an excellent source of information about what actually happens in classroom.
3. It is a study of an individual in a natural situation and is therefore more useful than the restricted study in a test situation.
4. The method can be used with children of all ages. Younger the child, the easiest it is to observe him. This method has been found very useful with shy children.
5. it can be used in every situation, physical- activities, workshop and classroom situations as well.
6. It is adaptable both to the individuals and the groups.

Although observation is regarded as an efficient method for psychological studies, students yet it suffers from the following drawbacks limitations:

Limitations:

1. There is great scope for personal prejudices and bias of the observer. The observer's interest, values can distort observation.

2. Records may not be written with hundred percent accuracy as the observations are recorded after the actions are observed. There is some time lag.
3. The observer may get only a small sample of study behavior. It is very difficult to observe everything that the student does or says. As far as possible observation should be made from several events.

4. It reveals the overt behavior only- behavior that is expressed and not that is within.
5. It lacks replicability as each natural situation can occur only once.

Students looking at the drawbacks an observation method have psychologists have suggested various guidelines to be followed for making good observation. So let us find out which are these essential guidelines for making good observation.

Essential guidelines for making good observation

1. Observe one individual at a time. It is desirable to focus attention on just one individual at a time in order to collect comprehensive data.
2. Have specific criteria for making observations. The purpose of making observation should be clear to the observe before he or she begins to observe so that the essential characteristics or the behavior of the person fulfilling the purpose can be noted.
3. Observations should be made over a period of time. To have a real estimate of the true behavior of a person it should be observed as frequently as possible. A single observation will not be sufficient to tell us that this is the characteristic of the individual.
4. The observations should be made in differing and natural situations in natural settings to increase its validity. For example, a pupil's behavior in the classroom may not be typical of him; therefore he should be observed in variety of settings to know the behavior most typical of the person.
5. Observe the pupil in the context of the total situation.
6. The observed facts must be recorded instantly, that is just at the time of their occurrence otherwise the observer may forget some of the facts and the recording may not be accurate.
7. It is better to have two or more observers.
8. Observations should be made under favorable conditions. The observer should be in position to clearly observe what he or she is observing. There should not be any undue distraction or

disturbances. One should also have an attitude free from any biases or prejudices against the individual being observed.

9. Data from observations should be integrated with other data. While arriving at the final conclusion about the individual, one should put together all that we know about the individual from the other sources then we can give an integrated and comprehensive picture of the individual.

These precautions must be borne in mind in order to have reliable observations.

Check Your Progress:

Note: a] Write your answer in the space given below:

b] Compare your answer with those given at the end:

2. A] Fill in the blanks:

1] Observation has been defined as '

"

B. Mention four types of observation:

1]

3]

2]

4]

C. List the steps involved in observation method:

1]

3]

2]

4]

4. EXPERIMENTAL METHODS

Students till now, we saw introspection method and observation method used in psychology of learning. But these methods lack scientific objectivity and validity. Experimental method is the most scientific and objective method of studying behavior. It is the method, which is responsible for assigning the status of Science to psychology. So let us learn more about this Experimental method.

In 1879, William Wundt established the first psychological laboratory at Leipzing in Germany. Since then experimental method in psychology has become popular, Experimental method consists of actions of actions performed under prearranged or rigidly controlled conditions.

Here the emphasis is on experimentation. Experimentation is where the investigator controls the educative factors to which a group of children are subjected during the period of inquiry and observes the resulting achievement.

J. W. Best describes, "Experimental research is the description and analysis of what will be, or what will occur under carefully controlled conditions."

Basic concepts /essentials of experimental method

a. Experiments are always conducted in laboratory. Hence the laboratory is essential.
b. Psychological experiments performed in this method essentially require two people; the experiment or group of experimenters who perform experiment and the other is the subject or subjects on whom the experiment is performed.
c. The key factor in this method is the controlling of conditions or variables. The term 'Variable' means that which can be varied or changed. By controlling. The variables we can eliminate the irrelevant conditions and isolate the relevant ones. We thus become able to observe the causal relationship between the phenomena keeping all other conditions almost constant. Let us understand this by and example. If we try to study the effect of intelligence on academic by the experimental method, we will need to determine the causative relation between the two phenomena (variables)- i.e. intelligence and academic achievement. One of these variables, the effect of which we want to study will be called the independent Variable and the other the dependent variable. Thus the independent variable stands for cause and the dependent variable is the effect of the cause. Other conditions like study-habits, sex, socio-eco conditions, parental education, home environment, health past learning,

memory etc. which exercise a good impact upon one's achievement besides one's intelligence are termed "interviewing variables". In Experimentation, all such interviewing variables are to be controlled, i.e. they are to be made constant or equalized and the effect of only one independent variable e.g. intelligence in present case, on one or more dependent variable is studied. The interviewing variables made constant, are hence called as controlled variables.

Steps in the experimental method

Students we have describe above, the basic concepts of experimental method. Here we will describe different steps, which are to be followed in conducting a typical experiment. These steps are as follows.

1. Raising a problem:

In any experiment the first steps is to identify a problem. For example it has been observed that the students cheat in the examinations. To stop it many recommend strict supervision.

But it has also been seen that even when there is strict supervision there is cheating, hence there crops up the problem of cheating under strict supervision or relaxed supervision. This problem may lead to experimentation.

2. Formulation of a hypothesis:

The next step in experimental method is the formulation of a hypothesis that "Strict supervision may lead to less copying in the examination as compared to the relaxed supervision. "This hypothesis is now to be tested by experiment.

3. Making a distinction between Independent and dependent variables:

In the example given above the cheating behavior of the students will be dependent variable while the nature of supervision will be the independent variable. It is because by changing the supervision the cheating behavior is expected change. In the present experiment we manipulate the conditions of supervision in order to discover the ways in which they determine the dependent variable that is the cheating behavior. We may observe the effect of supervision in the experimental situation and also the effect of relaxed supervision under similar conditions and with the same group of students.

4. Controlling the situational variables:

The experiment will not give valid results unless the situational variables are controlled. If the experiment is conducted with different set of students who have been trained in a different manner of have a different value system then the results will be different in comparison to those who have been subjected to experiment earlier. Similarly the other conditions like the person who is supervising the place of supervision etc. have to be controlled. This means that all those conditions, which might affect the dependent variable, are to e controlled. Since in any experiment there are numerous conditions which are needed to be controlled it is many a time difficult to do so. Hence we take recourse to various types of experimental designs, which we have described earlier.

5. Analysis of the Results:

Once the experiment is concluded the results are analysed. In our example we may apply simple percentages to find out in which type of supervision a higher percentage of students have copied. Many a times we apply more sophisticated statistics to analyse the results.

6. Verification of Hypothesis:

The last step in the experimental method is the verification of the hypothesis, which we have earlier framed. The result of the experiment exhibits whether the hypothesis which we have earlier framed. The result of the experiment exhibits whether the hypothesis is accepted of refuted. We may find that strict supervision leads to less copying. In that case we may conclude that our hypothesis is accepted. If the results are otherwise then our conclusion will be that the hypothesis is refuted.

Experimental Designs:

Students Experimental method is the most precise, planed, systematic and controlled method. It uses a systematic procedure called as experimental design. The term experimental design has tow different meanings one is the experimental design which represents the six basic steps we have referred above? Followed in an experiment. The second meaning of experimental design and selecting an appropriate statistical procedure. Experimental design provides important guidelines to the researcher to carry out his research study. Experimental design ensures adequate controls by avoiding irrelevant causes of variability. The layout of a design depends on the type of the problem the investigator wants to investigate. Students you should know that, no one design solves all the problems of a research study.

A variety of experimental designs have been developed by researchers in recent years. These designs differ as these are dependent upon:

a. the nature of problem
b. the situation
c. the subjects and their availability.

Let us study some of the experimental designs used while employing Experiment method.

Following are the samples of experimental designs.

A. One Group Design

1. One group posttest design: This type of design is the simplest ones. It is commonly called pre-experimental design. Students in such type of experiment no formal comparison is possible for there is no second group with comparison can be made. Let us illustrate with an example: suppose a teacher treats 10 students who are addicted to smoking in a period of three months. At the end of the period six students give up smoking. Such type of designs do not control any of the sources of invalidity.

2. One group pretest-posttest design: This is also simple design and is considered to be a rather poor design though better than one group posttest design. In this design the experimenter first tests a group on some aspects of behhaviour and then gives special treatment. He statistically analyses the data and calculates the difference between the pretest and posttest scores of the group.

The paradigm of the design is as follows:

Pretest

Independent variable

Posttest

T_1

X

T_2

Example, Suppose in the beginning of the semester, we administer test of educational psychology to students of MA education and then we teach them the subject through out the semester. At the end of the semester we administer posttest (T_2), and find out the difference between the scores on the initial and final tests.

B. Two Group Designs

Researches in education and psychology have often been criticized of being loosely controlled. In recent year more rigorous designs have been evolved by using statistics to make researches more scientific more scientific and objective.

Generally researchers use two parallel group techniques to see the effects of an independent variable on some dependent variable. Two group are equated on the basis of significant variable. One group called experimental and the other is called control group. The experimental group is subjected to a certain experience or to a specific treatment whereas the control group is not given any type of special treatment. After providing special treatment to the experimental group, both the groups are administered the same final test. The scores are statistically compared and conclusions are drawn as regards the effect of special treatment on the experimental group.

1. Randomized Control Group Pretest Posttest Design: The researcher in this design follows the procedure as given below.

   i. He selects subject by random method.
   ii. Assigns subjects to groups and X (Treatment) to groups by random method.
   iii. Tests the Ss on the dependent variable.
   iv. Keep all conditions the same for both the groups except for exposing the experimental S but not the control group to the independent variable for a specific time.
   v. Test the 'Ss' on the dependent variable.
   vi. Finds the difference between the two.
   vii. Compares the results to see whether the application of 'X' (treatment) caused a change in the experimental group.
   viii. Applies an appropriate statistical procedure.

2. Matched two group design. A matched two group design is a modification of the totally randomized two group design described above. In this design, both groups are matched in terms of some variable, the experimenter feels he would influence the dependent variable. Suppose we want to test the retention of two types of words closely associated and disassociated. We believe that I. Q. Will influence how well a person can retain words so we match the two groups on I. Q. Let us be more concrete to understand this point. Suppose there are ten subjects with I. Q. as follows:

C. Multi group Design with one Independent Variable (ANOVAR)

Two group paradigms are most common in education and psychology but events in nature do not always conveniently order into two groups. Some times the investigator has to compare the effect of different values of some variable or has to see the effect of several alternative variables on more than two groups. The procedure for carrying out one way analysis of variance (ANOVAR) is the same as for two group design. The distinguishing feature between the two types of investigation is the type of statistical analysis used.

D. Factorial Design

Factorial design is employed where more than one independent variables are involved in the investigation. Factorial designs may involves several factors.

E. Small N Design

We have briefly mentioned various experimental designs which are termed as large N group designs. In all large N group designs, the number of subject in classroom situation. In many instances, the psychologist or teacher is faced with situations in which large N is not possible, for example delinquency, problem of indiscipline etc. with the introduction of statistics in psychology, it is possible to conduct scientific research on small N group.

Merits of experimental method

Experimental method being most precise and scientific has following merits:

1. Experimental method is the most systematic method or getting reliable data.
2. Experimental method enables accurate observations due to controlled conditions.
3. It allows us to establish cause effect relationship between different phenomena.
4. The results obtained are valid and reliable.
5. The findings of the experimental method are verifiable by other experiments under identical conditions.
6. It helps to protect from the subjective opinions. Hence it provides objective information about the problem.
7. it provides adequate information about the problem.
8. In experimental method experiments are conducted under vigorously controlled conditions. The experimenter can control the application and withdrawal of independent variables.
9. Experimental method increases ones knowledge or psychological facts in child psychology, social and abnormal psychology.

It is rightly said the experimental method has made psychology a science.

Demerits of the method

Experimental method suffers from various following demerits:

1. Experimental method is costly and time consuming method as it requires a laboratory and apparatus to conduct it properly.
2. Experiments are conducted in artificially determined pattern of behavior. In real life situation it is quite different.
3. It needs specialized knowledge and therefore every teacher cannot be expected to conduct the experiment.
4. The scope is limited. All problems of psychology cannot be studied by this method as we cannot perform experiments for all the problems that may come up in the diverse subject matter of psychology.
5. Accurate measurements in case of human beings are never possible.
6. It is difficult to always control the independent variable therefore it is not possible to create desired conditions in laboratory.
7. It is not possible to reach certainty in matters of social science s including educational psychology.

Check Your Progress – 3

Note a) Write your answer in the space given below

b) Compare your answer with those given at the end.

3 A) Fill in the blanks:

1. established at the first psychological

laboratory at Leipzig in Germany.

2. Psychological experiments require two people.

They are a) b)

3. The key factor in the experimental method is the controlling of
4. Experimental method has three following variables

i.
ii.
iii.

B. List the steps involved in experimental method:

a.

d)

b. c)

e)f)

C. List the different experimental designs employed in experimental Method:

a.

d)

b. c)

e.

Conclusion:

Students we have learnt in the above unit the four methods of studying psychology of learning. But which of the above discussed methods is the best among other four is a difficult questions to be answered. All the four methods have their strengths and weakness and possess some unique characteristics, which make them highly specific for use in a particular situation. A wise psychologist should have a keen insight into the nature of his subjects as well as the conditions affecting his work and accordingly select a proper method or methods for the objectives. Study of the behavior of his subjects much depends upon the sincerity, honesty, ability and experience of the investigator, who should always try to keep himself as scientific and objective as possible and leave no stone unturned for the overall analysis for the behavior of the subject or nature of the phenomena of the study.

Unit End Exercises :

1. Fill in the blanks:

a. Introspection is method of self-observation.
b. The word introspection is made up to two Latin Words "Intro" & "Aspection".

2. A) Fill the blanks

1. Observation has been defined as "Measurements" without " Instruments".
2. Observation deals with the overt bahaviour of persons in appropriate situation.

B. The five types of observation

1. Natural observation 2) Participant observation

3) Non-participant observation 4) Structured observation

5) Unstructured observation.

C. The steps involved in observation methods are:

1. Observation of behavior
2. Recording the behavior observed
3. Analysis and interpretation of behavior
4. Generalization

3. A) Fill in the blanks:

1. William Wundt established the first psychological at Leipzig in Germany.
2. Psychological experiments required two people. They are a) Experimenter b) Observer
3. The key factor in the experimental method is the controlling of variables.
4. Experimental method has three following variable

i. Independent variable
ii. Dependent variable
iii. Controlled variable

B. The steps involved in experimental method are:

a. Raising ;a problem
b. Formulation of hypothesis
c. Making a distinction between independent and dependent variable
d. controlling the situational variables
e. Analysis of result

f. Verification of hypothesis

C. The different experimental design employed in experimental Method.

a. One group design
b. Two group design
c. Multi group with one –Independent variable (ANOVA)
d. Factorial design
e. Small N design

4. A) Fill in the blanks

i. Clinical method includes clinical-study where in-depth study of an individual is done.
ii. Clinical method employs both method of diagnosis and treatment in dealing with an individual case.

B. The different sources used for collecting information about the individual are:

i. Identifying data
ii. Environmental background
iii. developmental history
iv. History of exceptional behavior

C. The different ways in which the problem of an individual is diagnosed

i. Adequate physical checkup
ii. Making out the case history
iii. The clinical interview
iv. Direct observation of behavior
v. Using tests and measuring devices.

D. The two ways in which the changes are brought about in their behavior of the individual for treatment of his/her problem.

a. Modifying the environmental forces
b. Modifying the individuals attitude

Textual Questions:

1. Describe introspection method along with its merits and demerits?

2. How will you use the observation method to study child's behavior?
3. Discuss the essential guidelines for making good observations?
4. Discuss the merits and limitations of experimental method?
5. Why is experimental method considered excellent method of collecting data?
6. Describe fully the clinical method and bring out in detail the merits and limitations of this method?

????

CHAPTER-3

GROWTH AND DEVELOPMENT

Unit Structure

0. Learning Objectives
1. Introduction
2. Human Development
    1. The Concept of Growth and Development
    2. Principles of Growth and Development
3. Stages of Development
4. Developmental Characteristics of Children and Adolescents: Physical, Cognitive, Emotional and Social aspects
    1. Developmental Characteristics of Infancy (Birth to 2 Years)
    2. Developmental Characteristics of Early Childhood (Age 2- 6 Years)
    3. Developmental Characteristics of Late Childhood (Age 6- 12 Years)
    4. Developmental Characteristics of Adolescents (Age 12-18 Years)
5. Role of the Teacher in Facilitating Growth and Development
6. Let Us Sum Up
7. Suggested Readings

0. OBJECTIVES

This unit will help you learn the concept, the broad principles, the stages and developmental characteristics of growth and development. After going through this unit, you should be able to:

- Explain the concept of growth and development.
- Differentiate between growth and development.
- Explain the principles of growth and development.
- Describe the stages of human growth and development.
- Describe the characteristics of each stage of human growth and development.
- Discuss the educational implications of the principles of growth and development.
- Explain the role of the teacher in the facilitation of growth and development during adolescence.

1. INTRODUCTION

Human beings keep changing. During their lives, they change in size, appearance and psychological makeup. The way they change differs from individual to individual. However, the fundamental underlying patterns of growth and development remain more or less the same and take place in an orderly way. Each individual, with his unique heredity and the way he is nurtured, determines the way he traverses the broad highway of his life at his rate of progress. He will attain the size, shape, capacities and developmental status in a way, which is peculiar to him at each stages of life.

In this unit, we shall discuss the concept, principles and various stages of growth & development. Children differ in physical, cognitive, social, and emotional growth patterns. They also differ in the ways they interact with and respond to their environment as well as play, affection. Having an understanding of the sequence of growth and development prepares teachers to help and give attention to all the children.

2. HUMAN DEVELOPMENT

Can you recall events from your early childhood say the second or third year? You might have a few vague and blurred memories about your childhood. The experiences of that period form the basis of the type of person you are today. How human beings grow, change and adjust themselves to their environment is the focus of development and behavior as also the concepts, principles and theories of growth of development.

The human being is never static. From conception to death, he undergoes changes. There are progressive changes in response to environmental conditions. His body organs and psychological functions show the curves of capacity and achievement as well as slow erosion and decay. Cognitive abilities develop and then degenerate; basic metabolism reaches a peak, then declines, the endocrine function flourishes, and then fades. There is a rise and fall of physical energy in terms of both the force and speed of action with age. In fact, no organ or function of human beings has yet been found which is independent of age determinants.

At the time of conception, a child has genetic potentialities that are partly predictable and partly unpredictable. These genetic potentialities are determined by the nature of his biological inheritance. Still there is room for a tremendous range in the ways he uses the genetic potentialities, depending upon the environment that may help or hinder the development of those potentialities.

1. The Concept of Growth and Development

The terms growth and development are often used interchangeably. Actually, they are conceptually different. Neither growth nor development takes place all by itself.

Growth refers to quantitative changes in size, which include physical changes in height, weight, size, internal organs, etc. As an individual develops, old features like baby fat, hair and teeth, etc., disappear and new features like facial hair are acquired. When maturity comes, the second set of teeth, primary and secondary sex characteristics, etc., appear. Similar changes occur in all aspects of the personality. During infancy and childhood, the body steadily becomes larger, taller and heavier. To designate this change the term growth is used. Growth involves changes in body proportions as well as in overall stature and weight. The term growth thus indicates an increase in bodily dimensions. However, the rate of growth differs from one part of the body to the other.

Development, by contrast, refers to qualitative changes taking place simultaneously with quantitative changes of growth. It may be defined as a progressive series of orderly, coherent changes. The term progressive signifies that changes are directional, that they lead forward rather than backward. Orderly and coherent suggest that a definite relationship between the changes taking place and those that precede or will follow them. Development represents changes in an organism from its origin to its death, but more particularly the progressive changes that take place from origin to maturity.

Thus, development may be explained as the series of overall changes in an individual due to the emergence of modified structures and functions that are the outcome of the interactions and exchanges between the organism and its environment.

2. The Principles of Growth and Development

Following are the fundamental principles of growth and development.

i. Development follows a pattern or a sequence:

Development tends to proceed from the head downward. This is called the **cephalocaudal principle.** According to this principle, the child first gains control of the head, then the arms, then the legs. Infants gain

control of head and face movements within the first two months after birth. In the next few months, they are able to lift themselves up using their arms. By 6 to 12 months of age, infants start to gain leg control and may be able to crawl, stand, or walk.

Development also proceeds from the center of the body outward according to the **proximodistal principle.** Accordingly, the spinal cord develops before other parts of the body. The child's arms develop before the hands, and the hands and feet develop before the fingers and toes. Fingers and toes are the last to develop.

ii. **Development proceeds from general to specific responses:** It moves from a generalized to localized behavior. The newborn infant moves its whole body at one time instead of moving only one part of it. It makes random kicking with its legs before it

can coordinate the leg muscles well enough to crawl or to walk.

iii. Development is a continuous process:

Development does not occur in spurts. Growth continues from the moments of conception until the individual reaches maturity. It takes place at slow regular pace rather than by 'leaps and bounds'. Although development is a continuous process, yet the tempo of growth is not even, during infancy and early years growth moves swiftly and later it slacken.

iv. Different aspects of growth develop at different rates

Neither all parts of the body grow at the same rate nor do all aspects of mental growth proceed equally. They reach maturity at different times. Development also depends on maturation. **Maturation** refers to the sequence of biological changes in children. These orderly changes give children new abilities. Much of the maturation depends on changes in the brain and the nervous system. These changes assist children to improve their thinking abilities and motor skills. A rich learning environment helps children develop to their potential.

Children must mature to a certain point before they can gain some skills. For instance, the brain of a four-month-old has not matured enough to allow the child to use words. A four-month-old will babble and coo. However, by two years of age, with the help of others, the child will be able to say and understand many words. This is an example of how cognitive development occurs from simple tasks to more tasks that are complex. Likewise, physical skills develop from general to specific movements. For example, think about the way an infant waves its arms and legs. In a young infant, these movements are random. In several months, the infant will likely be able to grab a block with his or her whole hand. In a little more time, the same infant will grasp a block with the thumb and forefinger.

v. Most traits are correlated in development:

Generally, it is seen that the child whose intellectual development is above average is so in health size, sociability and special aptitudes.

vi. Growth is complex:

All of its aspects are closely interrelated. The child's mental development is intimately related to his physical growth and its needs.

vii. Growth is a product of the interaction of the organism and environment:

Among the environmental factors one can mention nutrition, climate the conditions in the home, the type of social organization in which individual moves and lives.

viii. There are wide individual differences in growth:

Individual differences in growth are caused by differences in heredity and environment.

ix. Growth is both quantitative and qualitative:

These two aspects are inseparable. The child not only grows in 'size'; he grows up or matures in structure and function too.

x. Development is predictable:

It is possible for us to predict at an early age the range within which the mature development of the child is likely to fall. However, mental development cannot be predicted with the same degree of accuracy.

Check Your Progress

1. Indicate 'G' for 'growth' and 'D' for 'development' for each of the following statements.

   a. A six-month-old baby shows signs of teething.
   b. A three-month-old baby begins to turn over and lie on its stomach.
   c. An infant begins to focus its eyes on an object dangling before it.
   d. A thirteen-year-old boy begins to have hair on his face.

2. Write 'T' for 'true' and 'F' for 'false' for the following statements.

   a. A child talking full sentences is part of development.
   b. The difference in height between two children is due to the different rates of their development

3. Differentiate between growth and development.

4. Describe briefly the principles of growth and development

3. STAGES OF DEVELOPMENT

Any development process proceeds through some stages and each development stage differs from the other. Each stage of development has its characteristic. Psychologists have separated human life span into stages or periods and identified specific changes that may be expected during each stage. The transition from one stage to the next is gradual rather than sudden. The age groups assigned to each stage of the development are general as shown in the Table 1.0.

Table 1.0 Stages of Development

Age Groups (Years)	**Stage of Development**	**Description of Each Stages**
Birth to 2	Infancy	**Neonate:** This stage is a period from birth to two weeks. **Babyhood:** This stage is of rapid growth and development. There are changes in body proportions as well as intellectual growth.
2 to 6	Early childhood	This is the preschool period. It is also called the pre-gang age. In this stage, the child seeks gain control over his environment. He also starts to learn to make social adjustment.
6 to 12	Late childhood	This is the primary school age. Here child is expected to acquire the rudiments of knowledge that are considered essential for successful adjustment to adult life. He/She are also expected to learn certain essential skills.
12 to 18	Adolescence	

This is the period of physiological change. It is the period when children become sexually mature. It is also the period of intensified personal interaction with peers of the same and opposite sex.

18 to 40

Young adulthood

The responsibilities of adulthood include important decisions like choosing a career, a life partner, etc. Young adulthood begins with setting goals and aspirations.

40 to 60

Middle adulthood

After settling down in thirties and having lived through with rooting phase, the individual starts feeling sense of uprooting and dissatisfaction during the forties. A physical decline in the form of wrinkles, thickening waistlines, greying and thinning hair start appearing. The changes are often termed middle life transition, middle- age revolt, mid-career crisis or middle-age slump. These terms point U, the loss of youth and the coming of old age. In women, hormonal changes of menopause (ending of menstruation) generate

anxiety and depression.

Over 60

Late adulthood

Aging is a process, which causes loss of vitality. Aged adults are more concerned about their health and death. Their visit to doctors is more frequent. Retirement has the worst impact on aged adults. They gradually lose their sense of meaningfulness in life. Some develop interests in social service and spend their time in financial planning, reading, travelling, visiting religious places and enjoying nature.

4. DEVELOPMENTAL CHARACTERISTICS OF CHILDREN AND ADOLESCENTS: PHYSICAL, COGNITIVE, EMOTIONAL AND SOCIAL ASPECTS

Children and adolescents grow and develop at very different rates. Each individual is unique, with a distinct personality and life experience. For this reason, age is not the only sign of where a particular child or adolescent is in terms of development. The different aspects of development are as follows.

- **Physical development** – genetic make-up, ethnicity, race, gender, nutrition and diet, exercise, sleep patterns, use of tobacco, alcohol or other drugs, stress and stressful life events, environmental toxins and socioeconomic status
- **Cognitive development** – academic setting, family environment, parent or caregiver involvement, access to early education opportunities, teacher support, personal motivation, gender and cultural or ethnic context
- **Emotional development** – individual temperament, parent and family relationships, support network, life experiences and transitions; media exposure and influence and a tendency toward risk-taking or delinquent behaviors
- **Social development** – peer influence, popularity, community and societal context

1. Developmental Characteristics of Infancy (Birth to 2 Years)

Physical Development

The development of control and mastery over one's own body in both gross and fine motor skills is the infant's primary physical task, culminating toward the end of the first year in walking.

The infant perfects the gross and fine motor skills that emerged during the first year by developing balance, coordination, stability, and an improved ability to manipulate objects.

Cognitive Development

Cognition begins with alertness, awareness, recognition, and interest in visual, auditory, and tactile (touch) stimuli. As motor development improves, the infant begins to explore and manipulate

objects and develops a rudimentary understanding of their properties. Infants develop ***object permanence*** toward the end of the first year.

- The emergence of symbolic thought is central to cognitive development. This results in the ability to understand and produce language.

Social Development

The most important social task is the development of attachment to the primary caretaker, most often the child's mother.

The child develops affectionate and trusting relationships with other family members and with adults outside the family. The child can also be engaged in simple games and play.

Emotional Development

The development of basic trust, a derivative of the positive attachment between the infant and the primary caretaker, occurs during the first year. This is a cornerstone of emotional development.

The primary developmental task involves the development of autonomy, which includes mastery and control over oneself and one's environment. Children develop a rudimentary self-concept, experiencing pride and pleasure at being "good" and embarrassment, shame, and distress at being "bad."

2. Developmental Characteristics of Early Childhood (2-6 Years)

Physical Development

The child develops increased strength and uses motor skills to master challenges in the environment, such as bicycles, stairs, balls, playground equipment, eating utensils, crayons, and other objects. The child is developmentally ready to master toilet training.

Most basic gross motor abilities have emerged. Existing skills are practiced and perfected, and the child develops mastery in applying motor skills to increasingly challenging and complex situations.

Cognitive Development

Perfection of language skills and the use of language to communicate with others is the principle cognitive task.

Language develops rapidly. Grammar and syntax are refined, and vocabulary increases geometrically. The child uses language as a communication tool. Thinking is concrete and egocentric in nature. Problem solving is illogical and magical thinking and fantasies are prevalent.

Social Development

The child develops rudimentary relationships with other children, which are usually characterized by "parallel play," that is playing in the presence of, rather than in interaction with, other children. Children also begin to imitate social roles at this time. Toilet training represents a significant internalization of social rules and expectations.

The child expands social relationships outside the family and develops interactive and cooperative play skills with peers. The child begins to understand, explore, imitate, and practice social roles. The child learns concepts of "right" and "wrong" and begins to understand the nature of rules. He experiences guilt when he has done something wrong.

Emotional Development

The preschool child has been described as "on the make." Erikson refers to the child's primary mode of operation during this stage as initiative. The child is intrusive, takes charge, is very curious and continually tries new things, actively manipulates the environment, and is self-directed in many activities. The child's ability to understand "right" and "wrong" leads to self-assessments and affects the development of self-esteem.

3. Developmental Characteristics of Late Childhood (Age 6- 12 Years)

Physical Development

The child practices, refines, and masters complex gross and fine motor and perceptual-motor skills.

Cognitive Development

Concrete operational thinking replaces egocentric cognition. The child's thinking becomes more logical and rational. The child develops the ability to understand others' perspectives.

Social Development

Relationships outside the family increase in importance, including the development of friendships and participation in a peer group. The child imitates, learns, and adopts age appropriate social roles, including those that are gender-specific. The child develops an understanding of rules. Rules are relied upon to dictate proper social behavior and to govern social relationships and activities.

Emotional Development

The child is industrious, purposeful, and goal directed in her activities. She is confident and self-directed. The child is developing a better sense of herself as an individual, with likes and dislikes and special areas of skill. She is capable of introspection. The child evaluates her worth by her ability to perform. Self-esteem is largely derived from one's perceived abilities.

4. Developmental Characteristics of Adolescence (Age 12- 18 Years)

Physical Development

Physiological changes at puberty promote rapid growth, the maturity of sexual organs, and development of secondary sex characteristics.

Cognitive Development

During early adolescence, precursors to formal operational thinking appear, including a limited ability to think hypothetically and to take multiple perspectives. During middle and late adolescence, formal operational thinking becomes well developed and integrated in a significant percentage of adolescents.

Social Development

Social relationships in early adolescence are centered in the peer group. Group values guide individual behavior. Acceptance by peers is critical to self-esteem. Most peer relationships are still same-sex.

Young adolescents become interested in sexual relationships, but most contact is through groups. Some youth may begin to experiment with sexual behavior, but many early adolescents are not sexually active with other youth. Social roles are still largely defined by external sources.

During middle and late adolescence, values become individualized and internalized after careful consideration and independent thought.

Friends are more often selected on personal characteristics and mutual interests. The peer group declines in importance, individual friendships are strengthened, and more youth "date" in one-on-one relationships. The youth experiments with social roles and explores options for career choice.

Emotional Development

The early adolescent is strongly identified with the peer group. Youth depend upon their peers for emotional stability and support and to help mold the youth's emerging identity. Self-esteem is greatly affected by acceptance of peers.

Early adolescents are emotionally labile with exaggerated affect and frequent mood swings. They are very vulnerable to emotional stress.

During middle and late adolescence, identity is more individualized, and a sense of self develops and stabilizes that is separate from either family or peer group. Self-esteem is influenced by the youth's ability to live up to internalized standards for behavior. Self-assessment and introspection are common.

Check Your Progress

1. Match the columns of physical development of the following stages:-

A B

1. Infancy a. considerable stability is attained.
2. Childhood b. Physical maturity attained at optimum level.
3. Adolescence c. Motor & neuromuscular coordination begins.

2) Match the stages:-

columns

of

social development of the following

A

1. Infancy

B

a. Radical outlook and questioning of

the social norms.

2. Childhood b. Social response directed towards family members.
3. Adolescence c. Social values, attitudes and interests

are developed.

2. What is a neonate?

a. A newborn baby b) An irritable baby c) An unloved baby.

d) An abnormal baby.

3. What are the main characteristics of a baby under the age of two or three years?
4. List the main points of physical development in adolescents.
5. Identify the three needs of early childhood.

5. ROLE OF THE TEACHER IN FACILITATING GROWTH AND DEVELOPMENT

What we know about the child is vast and impressive. However, what we do not know is even more vast and overwhelming. Every new insight opens up new questions. Therefore, as a teacher we need to update our knowledge about the problems of children, in the context of the media explosion, economic strivings, resultant social, cultural and value changes. With this, we will be able to make a reliable diagnosis and apply the knowledge of child psychology to better their adjustment with themselves and with the world around them.

We, as a teacher, should know what to expect from the child (student), and what he needs physically, socially and emotionally. The routine teacher-taught relationship would not benefit him unless the students are dealt with empathetically as a social being, as an individual self, and as a biological organism.

A teacher should accept and make our students accept the reality of physical and biological changes so that the transition takes a smooth course without causing any psychological disadvantage. We need to create such challenging conditions, which may lead to the effective coordination of physical, mental and other functions in order to ensure adequate adjustment to probable life situations. Yet another task that teacher should ensure is to secure effective and desirable responses, and prevent or eliminate ineffective or undesirable ones.

One way is to arrange conditions in a way that make desirable responses satisfying and not annoying. Positive training in self-direction and self-control should be given to students. Some of the following points should be kept in mind while guiding them:

- Control and guidance must come from the student himself under the teacher's supervision.
- Harsh, strict and unsympathetic control and prescription of every detail of conduct leaving no place, for self-control and self-direction are not conducive to student's mental health and adjustment to life's events.
- Proper guidance, rational shifts of treatment, and principles of autonomy should be judiciously applied to ensure smooth passage through the turbulent period of student.

It is around the adolescence stage that students reach the higher levels of their school education. A teacher need to receive adequate knowledge and skills with due preparedness in order to handle their emotional and social needs. As a teacher, we need to appreciate the fact that students at this stage are prone to revolt against established norms, rules, and authority. You should keep yourself ready to provide explanations and rationale for the beliefs and values, which your students would question. Students at this time need proper guidance to decide on the right course of action. They need supportive judgments to do things, which provide them self-confidence and self- assurance.

The range of individual differences in mental ability among adolescents is wide. You need to use some plan of classification to secure homogeneous groups in respect of significant abilities and achievements so that curricular and instructional needs can be suitably met. Studies have indicated that in certain tasks a student's performance would improve when others (teachers) are around. This phenomenon is called **social facilitation**. However, this is not a universal phenomenon. Still other studies have shown that when a student is first trying.

To learn something new, the presence of others is detrimental. In such a situation, the teacher has to assess the situation (considering the class as a social unit) and the personality traits of his students and accordingly he should facilitate their growth and development.

6. LET US SUM UP

In this unit, we have studied the concept of human growth and development. The stages of development and the characteristics of each stage have also been discussed. The

principles of development, their importance and need to study them scientifically have been discussed. As you have seen, adolescence is a period of transition between childhood and adulthood. Accompanying it is a number of problems. During this period, adolescents are considered neither as children nor as adults. Their status remains ambiguous. They are prone to rebel against authority. What as a teacher, we can do to attend to these problems and how we can help the development of a balanced personality of our student's have been dealt with in order to create a better understanding of students needs and problems.

Units End Exercises :

1. Trace those events from your own childhood and adolescence stages that reflect the characteristics of these periods.
2. "Adolescence is a period of storm and stress". Discuss with convincing arguments.
3. How can a teacher help adolescents develop a balanced personality? Discuss your experiences in this regard.
4. Describe the physical, emotional and social developmental characteristics of early and late childhood.

????

CHAPTER-4

LEARNING

Unit Structure

0. Learning Objectives
1. Introduction
2. Concept of learning (Meaning, Definition, Characteristics, Types)
3. Nature of learning
4. Process of learning
5. Learning curve

0. OBJECTIVES

After going through this unit, you will be able to:

- Explain the concept & nature of learning.
- Explain the steps involved in the process of learning.
- Tell the meaning & importance of learning curve.
- Explain the different types of learning curve.
- Describe the different stages of learning curve.
- Describe the different learning theories

1. INTRODUCTION

Dear students, what does the word "learning" bring to your mind? learning to read, to ride a bicycle, to act, to use a computer, to play synthesizer etc. Each one of us learns something or the other intentionally or accidentally. Learning situations are most natural and common in our life. Every moment you learn something or the other because of the varied experience you have in life. In the educational process, the central idea is learning.

You are aware of a child learns right from his birth and goes on learning throughout his lifetime. An infant is quite helpless at birth, but slowly he learns to adopt himself to the environment around him. E.g. A child approaches a burning matchstick; the child burns his hand and withdraws. Another time when he comes to a burning matchstick, he takes no time to withdraw himself away. He learns to avoid not only the burning matchstick but also all burning things.

When this happens, we say that the child has learned that if you touch a flame, you get burnt up. In this way, the change in the behavior of an individual occurs through direct or indirect experiences. This change in behavior brought about by experience is called as learning. This is a very simple explanation of the term learning. Now let us understand the meaning and definitions of learning.

2. CONCEPT OF LEARNING

Meaning and Definitions of learning

Learning, in psychology, the process by which a relatively lasting change in potential behavior occurs because of practice or experience. Learning is also a process of acquiring modifications in existing knowledge, skills, habits, or tendencies through experience, practice, or exercise.

Gates and others "Learning is the modification of behavior through experience"

Henry, P smith "Learning is the acquisition of new behavior or strengthening or weakening of old behavior as a result of experience".

Crow and Crow "Learning is the acquisition of habits, knowledge and attitudes. It involves new ways of doing things, and it operates in an individual's attempt to overcome obstacles or to adjust to new situations."

Skinner "Learning is the process of progressive behavior adaptation."

Munn"To learn is to modify behavior and experience."

M. L. Bigge "Learning may be considered as change in insights, behavior, perception, motivation or a combination of these."

The above definitions emphasize four attributes of learning...

- As Process: the first is that learning is permanent change in behavior.
- It does not include change due to illness, fatigue, maturation and use of intoxicant.
- The learning is not directly observable but manifests in the activities of the individual.
- Learning depends on practice and experience.

Characteristics of Learning

Yoakum & Simpson have stated the following general characteristics of learning: Learning is growth, adjustment, organization of experience, purposeful, both individual and social, product of the environment.

According to W.R Mc law learning has the following characteristics.

1. Learning is a continuous modification of behavior continues throughout life
2. Learning is pervasive. It reaches into all aspects of human life.
3. Learning involves the whole person, socially, emotionally & intellectually.
4. Learning is often a change in the organization of behavior.
5. Learning is developmental. Time is one of its dimensions.
6. Learning is responsive to incentives. In most cases positive incentives such as rewards are most effective than negative incentives such as punishments.
7. Learning is always concerned with goals. These goals can be expressed in terms of observable behavior.
8. Interest & learning are positively related. The individual learns bet those things, which he is interested in learning. Most bys find learning to play football easier than learning to add fractions.
9. Learning depends on maturation and motivation.

Types of Learning

Learning has been classified in many ways.

I. Informal, formal and non-formal learning: Depending on the way of acquiring it learning may be informal, formal or non-formal.

- Informal learning is incidental. It takes place throughout life. It is not planned.
- Formal learning is intentional and organized. It takes place in formal educational institution.
- Non-formal is also intentional & organized. It is flexible.

II. Individual or Group learning: Learning is called either individual or group learning depending upon the number of individuals involved in the learning process.

III. Another classification involves the types of activity involved

a. **Motor learning:** - when learning involves primarily the use of muscles it is called as motor learning. e.g.: learning to walk, to operate a typewriter

b. **Discrimination learning:** - Learning which involves the act of discrimination is called discrimination learning. e.g. infant discriminates between mother and aunt, milk and water.

c. **Verbal learning:** - when learning involves the use of words it is called as verbal learning.

d. **Concept learning:** - when learning involves the formation of concept it is called as concept learning.

e. **Sensory learning:** - when learning is concerned with perception and sense it is sensory learning.

- Check your progress

1. Define learning
2. What do you mean my learning?
3. Explain the concept of learning and state its characteristics.
4. Write the different types of learning.

3. NATURE OF LEARNING

a. **Learning is adaptation or adjustment:** Friends, we all continuously interact with our environment. We often make adjustment and adapt to our social environment. Through a process of continuous learning, the individual prepares himself for necessary adjustment or adaptation. That is why learning is also described as a process of progressive adjustment to ever changing conditions, which one encounters.

b. **Learning is improvement:** Learning is often considered as a process of improvement with practice or training. We learn many things, which help us to improve our performance.

c. **Learning is organizing experience:** Learning is not mere addition of knowledge. It is the reorganization of experience.

d. **Learning brings behavioral changes:** Whatever the direction of the changes may be, learning brings progressive changes in the behavior of an individual. That is why he is able to adjust to changing situations.

e. **Learning is active:** Learning does not take place without a purpose and self-activity. In any teaching learning process, the activity of the learner counts more than the activity of a teacher.

f. **Learning is goal directed:** when the aim and purpose of learning is clear, an individual learns immediately. It is the purpose or goal, which determines what, the learner sees in the learning situations and how he acts. If there is no purpose or goal learning can hardly be seen.

g. **Learning is universal and continuous:** All living creatures learn. Every moment the individual engages himself to learn more and more. Right from the birth of a child till the death learning continues.

4. PROCESS OF LEARNING

Learning is a process. It is carried out through steps. Learning process involves –

a. A motive or a drive.
b. An attractive goal.
c. A block to the attainment of the goal.

Let us see the steps one by one –

a. **A motive or a drive:** Motive is the dynamic force that energizes behavior and compels an individual to act. We do any activity because of our motives or our needs. When our need is strong, enough we are compelled to strive for its satisfaction. Learning takes place because of response to some stimulation. As long as our present behavior, knowledge, skill and performance are adequate to satisfy all our needs, use do not feel any necessity to change our behavior or acquire new knowledge and skills. It is this requirement, which initiates a learner to learn something.

b. **Goal:** Every individual has to set a definite goal for achievement. We should always have a definite goal for achieving anything. If a definite goal is set then learning becomes purposeful and interesting.

c. **Obstacle /block /barrier:** The obstacle or block or the barrier is equally important in the process of learning. The obstacle or the barriers keep us away from attaining the goal.

Now, you will think how the obstacle can be important in the process of learning. So let me tell you, if you face no difficulty of any kind in attaining the goal, you will not bring any change in your present behavior or stock of knowledge or skills. Thus, the block or the barrier is an essential step in the learning process.

Let us clear the above views by taking an example. Suppose you wish to be included in your college hockey team. You want to have the esteem of your colleagues, your teachers. You are also motivated try the interesting experiences that you many enjoy. But you are blocked by your lack of skill in dodging, tackling and handling the ball. The obstacles in the path of goal achievement will set you make up your deficiency and acquire essential skill through sufficient practice and coaching.

Check Your Progress

1. Explain the nature of learning.
2. Explain the process of learning

5. LEARNING CURVE

Learning curve is a graphic representation of how learning takes place in a particular situation. In all type of learning situations, the course of learning can be depicted and described graphically by drawing learning curves against x and y axis.

The above figure shows a typical learning curve of many types of learning. The curve consists of a number of irregularities, as the progress is not constant.

For the convenience, the curve is divided into 5 stages – a, b, c, d and e.

a. **Period of slow progress:** Generally, when a person has to start a learning of a given activity from a scratch, his early progress will be slow. E.g., an infant's progress in learning to walk is very negligible in the beginning.

b. **Period of rapid progress:** In this stage, the learner's output raises rapidly. e.g. In typing once the learner has developed co ordination of the movement of fingers he shows rapid progress.

c. **Period of no apparent progress:** Learning curves frequently display a period of no apparent progress. It is also known as plateau. A period of no visible learning progress, preceded and followed by improvement is called as plateaus. E.g. In typing, a person may after having made rather consistent progress for some time, reach a point where perhaps for weeks no further progress is made.

Causes of plateau

i. The learner may be reorganizing the previous learning into a new pattern before further progress is possible.
ii. The learner may have hit upon bad habits
iii. Lack of progress may be due to decrease in motivation.
iv. The task may not be of uniform difficulty.
v. Loss of interest.
vi. The onset of fatigue is also one of the causes of a plateau.

d. **Period of sudden rise:** At the end of a plateau, there is generally a spurt in achievement. While on the plateau, the learner acquires better techniques, which help him later on to show rapid progress.

e. **Levelling:** All learning will finally slow down to such an extent that it will ultimately reach a period of no improvement. No one can continue to improve indefinitely in any given situation. The learning curve will eventually reach a limit, where no further improvement is possible. This limit is known as physiological limit.

1. Characteristics of Learning Curve.

i. Slow initial progress.
ii. Spurt-like learning after some time.
iii. Declination in the rate of learning.
iv. Plateaus of learning.
v. Sudden increase in learning.
vi. Gradual levelling at the end.

2. Types of Learning Curve.

We get different types of learning curves depending upon –

a. The nature of the learner
b. The nature of the task/learning material
c. Time available.
d. Conditions under which the learning takes place.

It is difficult to classify these learning curves. However, three common types of curves are there,

i. Negatively accelerated or the convex curve.
ii. Positively accelerated learning curve or the concave curve.
iii. Combination of convex-concave curve.

Convex curve

It depicts rapid initial improvement in learning that slows down with time. When the task is simple and the learner has previous practice on a similar task, we get this type of learning curve.

Concave curve

There is slow initial improvement and learning increases with time. When the task is difficult we get such type of learning curve.

Combination of convex concave curve

It looks like the capital letter 'S'. The curve takes concave or convex shape in the beginning depending upon the nature of the task.

In actual practical situations, such smooth curves are rarely found. Usually there are ups and downs (fluctuation).

3. Educational importance of learning curve

1. In acquiring the basic skills in various subjects, the learner at times appears to show no progress. At such moments, the teacher can diagnose the reasons for the lack of progress.
2. A student's progress may be arrested because the work is too complex for him. The teacher can observe the student's work and detect the part that gives him trouble. The teacher should see if the student has developed any faulty study habits, which impede his progress.
3. The plateau may be due to the lack of motivation. The teacher should provide encouragement in order to maintain motivation at a high level.
4. The learning curves give a graphic evidence of one's progress, which is an effective motivational device for the learner.
5. Occurrence of plateaus can be minimized by using superior teaching methods.

Unit End Exercise:

1. What is a learning curve?
2. Describe a typical learning curve.
3. What are the different types of learning curve?

4. State any two causes of plateau
5. Explain the educational importance of a learning curve.
6. State the important characteristics of a learning curve.

????

CHAPTER-5

LEARNING THEORIES

Unit Structure:

0. Objective
1. Learning Theories
2. Transfer of Training
3. Let us sum up
4. Suggested Reading

0. OBJECTIVE

After going through this unit, you will be able to :

- Explain the different types of learning curve.
- Describe the different stages of learning curve.
- Describe the different learning theories

1. LEARNING THEORIES

Learning as a process focuses on what happens when the learning takes place. Explanations of what happens constitute **learning theories.** A **learning theory** is an attempt to describe how people and animals learn, thereby helping us understands the inherently complex process of learning. **Learning theories** have two chief values according to Hill (2002). One is in providing us with vocabulary and a conceptual framework for interpreting the examples of learning that we observe. The other is in suggesting where to look for solutions to practical problems. The theories do not give us solutions, but they do direct our attention to those variables that are crucial in finding solutions.

The three main categories or philosophical frameworks under which learning theories fall is behavioral, cognitive, and constructivism. Behaviorism focuses only on the objectively observable aspects of learning. Cognitive theories look beyond behavior to explain brain-based learning. In addition, constructivism views learning as a process in which the learner actively constructs or builds new ideas or concepts.

We will discuss the behavioral theories under two broad categories: S-R theories.

- S-R (Stimulus-Response) theory with reinforcement

- E.L Thorndike- Trial and Error theory
- B.F Skinner- Operant Conditioning

- S-R (Stimulus-Response) theory without reinforcement

- Pavlov- Classical Conditioning

1. S-R (Stimulus-Response) theory with reinforcement

A. E.L Thorndike- Trial and Error Theory of Learning:

Edward Lee Thorndike (1874-1949) was the first American psychologist who put forward the Trial and Error Theory of learning. According to Thorndike, all learning takes place because of formation of bond or connection between stimulus and response. He further says that learning takes place through a process of approximation and correction. A person makes a number of trials, some responses do not give satisfaction to the individual but he goes on making further trials until he gets satisfactory responses. Thorndike conducted a number of experiments on animals to explain the process of learning. His most widely quoted experiment is with a cat placed in a puzzle box.

Thorndike put a hungry cat in a puzzle box. The box had one door, which could be opened by manipulating a latch of the door. A fish was placed outside the box. The cat being hungry had the motivation of eating fish outside the box. However, the obstacle was the latch on the door. The cat made random movements inside the box indicating trial and error type of behavior biting at the box, scratching the box, walking around, pulling and jumping etc. to come out to get the food. Now in the course of her movements, the latch was manipulated accidently and the cat came out to get the food. Over a series of successive trials, the cat took shorter and shorter time, committed less number of errors, and was in a position to manipulate the latch as soon as it was put in the box and learnt the art of opening the door.

Thorndike concluded that it was only after many random trials that the cat was able to hit upon the solutions. He named it as Trial and Error Learning. An analysis of the learning behavior of the cat in the box shows that besides trial and error the principles of goal, motivation, explanation and reinforcement are involved in the process of learning by Trial and Error.

- Laws of Learning

Based on Trial and Error Learning Theory, Thorndike gave certain laws of Learning. We shall discuss three fundamental Laws of Learning in this section. These laws are:

1. Law of Readiness

This law refers to the fact that learning takes place only when the learner is prepared to learn. No amount of efforts can make the child learn if the child is not ready to learn. The dictum that 'you can lead a horse to the pond but you can't make it drink water unless it feels thirsty' goes very well with this law. In other words, if the child is ready to learn, he/she learns more quickly, effectively and with greater satisfaction than if he/she is not ready to learn. In the words of Thorndike the three stages of this Law of Readiness are :

- For a conduction unit ready to conduct, to conduct is satisfying.
- For a conduction unit ready to conduct, not to conduct is annoying.
- For a conduction unit not ready to conduct, to conduct is annoying.

Thus, the Law of Readiness means mental preparation for action. It is not to force the child to learn if he is not ready. Learning failures are the result of forcing the learner to learn when he is not ready to learn something.

Educational Implications of Law of Readiness:

The law draws the attention of teacher to the motivation of the child. The teacher must consider the psycho-biological readiness of the students to ensure successful learning experiences. Curriculum / Learning experiences should be according to the mental level of maturity of the child. If this is not so, there will be poor comprehension and readiness may vanish.

2. Law of Exercise

This law explains the role of practice in learning. According to this law, learning becomes efficient through practice or exercise. The dictum 'Practice makes a man perfect' goes very well with this law. This law is further split into two parts — Law of use and Law of disuse. The law of use means that a connection between a stimulus and response is strengthened by its occurrence, its exercise or its use.

In other words, the use of any response strengthens it, and makes it more prompt, easy and certain. Regarding the law of disuse, it is said that when a modifiable connection is not made between a stimulus and a response over a length of time, the strength of that connection is decreased. This means that any act that is not practised for some time gradually decays. Anything that is not used exercised or practised for a certain period tends to be forgotten or becomes weak in strength, efficiency and promptness.

Educational Implications

Exercise occupies an important place in learning. Teacher must repeat, give sufficient drill in some subjects like mathematics, drawing, music or vocabulary for fixing material in the minds of the students. Thorndike later revised this law of exercise and accordingly it is accepted that practice does bring improvement in learning but it in itself is not sufficient.

Always practice must be followed by some reward or satisfaction to the learner. The learner must be motivated to learn.

3. Law of Effect

This is most important of Thorndike's laws, which state that when a connection between stimulus and response is accompanied by satisfying state, its strength is increased. On the other hand, when a connection is accompanied by an annoying state of affairs, its strength is reduced or weakened. The saying 'nothing succeeds like success' goes very well with this law. In other words, the responses that produce satisfaction or comfort for the learner are strengthened and responses that produce annoyance or discomfort for the learner are weakened. Thorndike revised this law in 1930 and according to this revision, he stated that reward strengthened the response but punishment did not always weaken the response. Then he placed more emphasis on the reward aspect than on the punishment aspect of Law of Effect.

Educational Implications

This law signifies the use of reinforcement or feedback in learning. This implies that learning trials must be associated with satisfying consequences. The teacher can use rewards to strengthen certain responses and punishment to weaken others. However, the use of reward is more desirable than the use of punishment in school learning. The teacher for motivating the students for learning situations can exploit the use of reward.

Check Your Progress

1. Define Learning. Describe E.L.Thorndike Trial & Error theory of learning.
2. Explain the Laws of learning given by E.L.Thorndike.

B. B.F.Skinners- Operant Conditioning What Is Operant Conditioning?

Operant conditioning (sometimes referred to as ***instrumental conditioning***) is a method of learning that occurs through rewards and punishments for behavior. Through operant conditioning, an association is made between a behavior and a consequence for that behavior.

Behaviorist B.F. Skinner coined the term operant conditioning, which is why it is also referred as Skinnerian conditioning. As a behaviorist, Skinner believed that internal thoughts and motivations could not be used to explain behavior. Instead, he suggested, we should look only at the external, observable causes of human behavior.

Skinner used the term *operant* to refer to any "active behavior that operates upon the environment to generate consequences" (1953). In other words, Skinner's theory explained how we acquire the range of learned behaviors we exhibit each and every day.

Skinner is regarded as the father of Operant Conditioning, but his work was based on Thorndike's law of effect. Skinner introduced a new term into the Law of Effect - Reinforcement. Behavior that is reinforced tends to be repeated (i.e. strengthened); behavior that is not reinforced tends to die out-or be extinguished (i.e. weakened).

Skinner studied operant conditioning by conducting experiments using animals, which he placed in a "*Skinner Box*" which was similar to Thorndike's puzzle box.

The Skinner box involved placing an animal (such as a rat or pigeon) into a sealed box with a lever that would release food when pressed. If food was released every time the rat pressed the lever, it would press it more and more because it learnt that doing so gives it food. Lever pressing is described as an operant behavior, because it is an action that results in a consequence. In other words, it operates on the environment and changes it in some way. The food that is released as a result of pressing the lever is known as a reinforcer, because it causes the operant behavior (lever pressing) to increase. Food could also be described as a conditioned stimulus because it causes an effect to occur.

Note: There is an important difference between a reward and a reinforcer in operant conditioning.

- A reward is something, which has value to the person giving the reward, but may not necessarily be of value to the person receiving the reward.
- A reinforcer is something, which benefits the person receiving it, and so results in an increase of a certain type of behavior.

Skinner identified three types of responses or operant that can follow behavior.

- **Neutral operants:** Responses from the environment that neither increase nor decrease the probability of a behavior being repeated.

- Reinforcersare any event that strengthens or increases the behavior it follows. There are two kinds of reinforcers.

1. Positive reinforcersare favorable events or outcomes that are presented after the behavior. In situations that reflect positive

2. reinforcement, a response or behavior is strengthened by the addition of something, such as praise or a direct reward.
3. Negative reinforcersinvolve the removal of an unfavorable events or outcomes after the display of a behavior. In these situations, a response is strengthened by the removal of something considered unpleasant.

In both of these cases of reinforcement, the behavior **increases.**

- Punishmentis the presentation of an adverse event or outcome that causes a decrease in the behavior it follows. Punishment weakens behavior. There are two kinds of punishment:

1. Positive punishment, sometimes referred to as punishment by application, involves the presentation of an unfavorable event or

outcome in order to weaken the response it follows.

2. Negative punishment, also known as punishment by removal, occurs when an favorable event or outcome is removed after a behavior occurs.

In both of these cases of punishment, the behavior **decreases.** Schedules of Reinforcement:

Intermittent reinforcement - reinforcement is given only part of the times the animal gives the desired response.

Continuous reinforcement - reinforcement is given every time the animal gives the desired response.

Ratio reinforcement - a pre-determined proportion of responses will be reinforced.

Fixed ratio reinforcement - reinforcement is given on a regular ratio, such as every fifth time the desired behavior is produced.

Variable (random) fixed reinforcement- reinforcement is given for a predetermined proportion of responses, but randomly instead of on a fixed schedule.

Interval reinforcement- reinforcement is given after a predetermined period of time.

Fixed interval reinforcement - reinforcement is given on a regular schedule, such as every five minutes.

Variable interval reinforcement - reinforcement is given after random amounts of time have passed.

In animal studies, Skinner found that continuous reinforcement in the early stages of training seems to increase the rate of learning. Later, intermittent reinforcement keeps the response going longer and slows extinction.

Skinner specifically addressed the applications of behaviorism and operant conditioning to educational practice. He believed that the goal of education was to train learners in survival skills for self and society. The role of the teacher was to reinforce behaviors that contributed to survival skills, and extinguish behaviors that did not. Behaviorist views have shaped much of contemporary education in children and adult learning.

Implication of the theory of operant conditioning:

1. **Conditioning study behavior**: Teaching is the arrangement of contingencies of reinforcement, which expedite learning. For

effective teaching teacher should arranged effective contingencies of reinforcement. Example: For Self learning of a student teacher should reinforce student behavior through variety of incentives such as prize, medal, smile, praise, affectionate patting on the back or by giving higher marks.

2. **Conditioning and classroom behavior:** During learning process child acquire unpleasant experiences also. This unpleasantness becomes conditioned to the teacher, subject and the classroom and learner dislikes the subject and a teacher. Suitable behavioral contingencies, atmosphere of recognition, acceptance, affection and esteem helps child in approaching teacher and the subject. If student is not serious in study, teacher make use of negative reinforcement like showing negligence, criticizing student etc. but if student is serious in study, teacher make use of positive reinforcement like prize, medal, praise and smile.

3. **Managing Problem Behavior:** Two types of behavior are seen in the classroom is undesired behavior and problematic behavior. Operant conditioning is a behavior therapy technique that shape students behavior. For this teacher should admit positive contingencies like praise, encouragement etc. for learning. One should not admit negative contingencies. Example punishment (student will run away from the dull and dreary classes – escape stimulation.

4. **Dealing with anxieties through conditioning:** Through conditioning fear, anxieties, prejudices, attitudes, perceptual meaning develops. Examples of anxiety are signals on the road, siren blown during wartime, child receiving painful injection from a doctor. Anxiety is a generalized fear response. To break the habits of fear, a teacher should use desensitization techniques. Initially teacher should provide very weak form of conditioned stimulus. Gradually the strength of stimulus should be increased.

5. **Conditioning group behavior:** Conditioning makes entire group learn and complete change in behavior is seen due to reinforcement. It breaks undesired and unsocial behavior too. Example: Putting questions or telling lie to teachers will make teachers annoyed in such circumstances students learn to keep mum in the class. Asking questions, active participation in class discussion will make the teacher feel happy – interaction will increase and teaching learning process becomes more effective.

6. **Conditioning and Cognitive Processes:** Reinforcement is given in different form, for the progress of knowledge and in the feedback form. When response is correct, positive reinforcement is given. Example: A student who stands first in the class in the month of January is rewarded in the month of December. To overcome this Programme instruction is used. In this subject matter is broken down into steps. Organizing in logical sequence helps in learning. Each step is build upon the preceding step. Progress is seen in the process of learning. Immediate reinforcement is given at each step.

7. **Shaping Complex Behavior:** Complex behavior exists in form of a chain of small behavior. Control is required for such kind of behavior. This extended form of learning is shaping technique. Smallest Behavior is controlled at initial stage. On behalf of different contingencies, next order of chain of behaviors is controlled. Example: Vocabulary in English. Teaching spelling is mainly a process of shaping complex form of behavior.

- Check Your Progress

1. What is Operant Conditioning? Describe theory operant conditioning given by B.F.Skinners with appropriate illustration.
2. Define reinforcement. What are the various schedules of reinforcement? Explain with examples.
3. Discuss the theory of operant conditioning and point out its implication to education

2. S-R (Stimulus-Response) theory without reinforcement

- Pavlov- Classical Conditioning (1849-1936)

Classical conditioning is a term used to describe learning which has been acquired through experience. One of the best-known examples of classical conditioning can be found with the Russian psychologist Ivan Pavlov and his experiments on dogs.

In these experiments, Pavlov trained his dogs to salivate when they heard a bell ring. In order to do this he first showed them food, the sight of which caused them to salivate.

Later Pavlov would ring a bell every time he would bring the food out, until eventually, he could get the dogs to salivate just by ringing the bell and without giving the dogs any food.

In this simple but ingenious experiment, Pavlov showed how a reflex (salivation, a natural bodily response) could become conditioned (modified) to an external stimulus (the bell) thereby creating a conditioned reflex/response.

Components Involved In Classical Conditioning

We can gain a better understanding of classical conditioning by looking at the various components involved in his experiment;

- The unconditioned stimulus.(UCS)
- The conditioned stimulus.(CS)
- The unconditioned reflex/response.(UCR)
- The conditioned reflex/response. (CR)

So let's look at each of these classical conditioning components in more detail now.

Note: In its strictest definition classical conditioning is described as a previously neutral stimulus which causes a reflex (stimulus means something which causes a physical response).

The Unconditioned Stimulus (food): (UCS) An unconditioned stimulus is anything, which can evoke a response without prior learning or conditioning.

For example, when a dog eats some food it causes his mouth to salivate. Therefore the food is an unconditioned stimulus, because it causes a reflex response (salivation) automatically and without the dog having to learn how to salivate.

Unconditioned Stimulus – This causes an automatic reflex response.

Conditioned Stimulus (bell): (CS) The conditioned stimulus is created by learning, and therefore does not create a response without prior conditioning.

For example, when Pavlov rang a bell and caused the dogs to salivate, this was a conditioned stimulus because the dogs learnt to associate the bell with food. If they had not learnt to associate the bell with food, they would not have salivated when the bell was rung.

Conditioned Stimulus – You need to learn first before it creates a response. It is an acquired power to change something.

Unconditioned Reflex/Response (salivation): (UCR) An unconditioned reflex is anything that happens automatically without you having to think about it, such as your mouth salivating when you eat. Unconditioned Reflex – Reflex that happens automatically and you did not have to learn how to do it.

Conditioned Reflex (salivation in response to bell): (CR) A conditioned reflex is a response which you have learnt to associate with something.

For example, the dogs salivated when Pavlov rang a bell, when previously (without conditioning) the bell would not cause the dogs to salivate.

Conditioned Reflex – A reflex that can be evoked in response to a conditioned stimulus (a previously neutral stimulus).

- Basic concepts in classical conditioning:

There are several principles that are associated with classical conditioning, some of these are:

- **Extinction:** a conditioned response will disappear over time when the conditioned stimulus is no longer presented.
- **Spontaneous recovery:** sometimes there is the weak appearance of a previously extinguished response.
- **Stimulus generalization:** this is when individuals respond in this same way to experience stimuli. For example, all fuzzy animals scaring a young child instead of just a fuzzy cat.
- **Stimulus discrimination:** organisms can learn to discriminate between various stimuli.
- **Higher order conditioning:** this is when a neutral stimulus can cause the conditioned response sense if it had been associated with the conditioned stimulus.

Types of classical conditioning

Forward conditioning: Learning is fastest in forward conditioning. During forward conditioning the onset of the conditioned stimulus (CS) precedes the onset of the unconditioned stimulus (US). Two common forms of forward conditioning are delay and trace conditioning.

Delay conditioning: In delay, conditioning the conditioned stimulus (CS) is presented and is overlapped by the presentation of the unconditioned stimulus (US).

Trace conditioning: During trace conditioning, the conditioned stimulus (CS) and US do not overlap. Instead, the conditioned stimulus (CS) is presented, a period is allowed to elapse during which no stimuli are presented, and then the unconditioned stimulus (US) is presented. The stimulus-free period is called the *trace interval*. It may also be called the *conditioning interval*.

Simultaneous conditioning: During simultaneous conditioning, the conditioned stimulus (CS) and unconditioned stimulus (US) are presented and terminated at the same time.

Backward conditioning: Backward conditioning occurs when a conditional stimulus (CS) immediately follows an unconditional stimulus (US). Unlike traditional conditioning models, in which the conditional stimulus (CS) precedes the unconditional stimulus (US), the conditional response (CR) tends to be inhibitory. This is because the conditional stimulus (CS) serves as a signal that the unconditional stimulus (US) has ended, rather than a reliable method of predicting the future occurrence of the unconditional stimulus (US).

Temporal conditioning: The unconditioned stimulus (US) is presented at regularly timed intervals, and CR acquisition is dependent upon correct timing of the interval between unconditioned stimulus (US) presentations. The background, or context, can serve as the conditioned stimulus (CS) in this example.

Unpaired conditioning: The conditioned stimulus (CS) and unconditioned stimulus (US) are not presented together. Usually they are presented as independent trials that are separated by a variable, or pseudo-random, interval. This procedure is used to study non-associative behavioral responses, such as sensitization.

CS-alone extinction: The conditioned stimulus (CS) is presented in the absence of the unconditioned stimulus (US). This procedure is usually done after the conditional response (CR) has been acquired through "forward conditioning" training. Eventually, the conditional response (CR) frequency is reduced to pre-training levels. Essentially, the stimulus is presented until habituation occurs.

Implications of Pavlov's Theory to Classroom Situations

1. The theory believed that one must be able to practice and master a task effectively before embarking on another one. This means that a student needs to be able to respond to a particular stimulus (information) before he/she can be associated with a new one.

2. Teachers should know how to motivate their students to learn. They should be versatile with various strategies that can enhance effective participation of the students in the teaching- learning activities.
3. Most of the emotional responses can be learned through classical conditioning. A negative or positive response comes through the stimulus being paired with. For example, providing the necessary school material for primary school pupils will develop good feelings about school and learning in them, while, punishment will discourage them from attending the school.

Check Your Progress

1. Define Classical Conditioning Theory
2. What is the meaning of Extinction Stage in Classical Conditioning?
3. Explain the meaning of Salivation in Pavlov's Theory of Classical Conditioning

4. What is the meaning of Unconditioned Response in Pavlov's Theory?

Conclusion

It is believed that the learners and more importantly the teachers have greatly benefited from all the theories. The teachers should be familiar with this theory and apply it to teaching-learning activities where applicable.

2. TRANSFER OF TRAINING

Introduction

The ability of the individual to apply the previous experience on the new related experience is what we call transfer of learning. Except students are able to transfer prior skills and knowledge on new ones, the continuity of learning will be difficult.

This unit will explain how old learning can be transferred to a new one. You will know what the classroom teacher needs to do in order to facilitate transfer of experiences among his/her students.

The essence of learning is that a previously learnt fact should be linked with a present experience. This is because human being must be dynamic and that the prior experience will make them to develop the new skills and knowledge. The influence the past experience has on the succeeding experience is called transfer of learning.

Cormier and Hagman, (1987) define transfer of learning as the application of skills and knowledge learned in one context being applied in another context.

Oladele (1998) defines transfer of learning as the effect of prior learning on the present. Learning is meaningful when the past learning smoothens the progress of something else. For example, if a learned experienced refuses to aid the new learning, the goal of training has seized to be accomplished. In the school, the teacher teaches some subjects in order that the experience gained in those subjects could be transferred into another.

Charham (1987) affirms that human and animal learning is normally affected by the past experience, and that the various subjects are included in the school curriculum because of their utility and wide application to real life situations For instance, the teacher who has taught his/her students some skills in Mathematics would believe that such skills be transferred to related subjects like Physics or Accounting. If the students fail to apply these skills in their subsequent learning, it means that the students have not been successful in transferring the learning.

The above example gives us clues into the different types of transfer of learning that we have. These are explained below:

a. **Positive Transfer:** This is a situation whereby a previously learnt fact or information aids in the understanding of a new task. Aside from aiding the learners in their subsequent learning, it also helps the learners to learn better and effectively the new task.

b. **Negative Transfer:** This is a type of learning in which prior experience imparts negatively on the new one. In this case, the understanding of past skills inhibits the mastering of new ones. For example, if a student wrongly connects information, it can lead to negative transfer.

c. **Zero Transfer:** This type of learning reveals no link between the previously learnt task and the recent one. The evidence of zero transfer is hardly seen, it reveals no clear positive or negative effect.

Theories of Transfer of Learning

a. **Theory of Mental Faculties:** This theory was propounded by the Greek Philosophers, notable among them was Aristotle. The basic tenet of the theory is that human mind is sub-divided into different powers of faculties like memory, judgment, reasoning or thinking. It is therefore believed that each of these faculties is reinforced and developed by cast and continuous memorization of poetry/poem and similar works. This theory believes that exercises and regular practice will strengthen the mental faculties. The theory therefore dismisses the concept of transfer of learning, to it a well-trained and disciplined mind is the ingredient needed for understanding of new information.

b. **Theory of Identical Elements:** The theory which was developed by the duo of Thorndike and Woodworth (American Psychologists) indicates that it is possible for an individual to transfer the prior skills and knowledge to recent ones because both experiences are identical (share things in common). This theory suggests that a successful or effective learning will happen if there are connections or interrelatedness between the old and the new experiences. For example, it is expected that a student who has learnt about anatomical parts of human being in a Biology lesson, should be able to do well when he/she is asked to name anatomical parts of a goat during Agriculture lesson.

c. **Theory of Generalization:** This theory was advocated by a Psychologist named Charles Judd. The assumption of the theory is that general principles aid transfer of learning better than segregated facts. This theory believes in Gestalt, an assertion which views learning from a whole or complete form rather than in isolated form. For example, the theory of generalization indicates that a learnt experience should be useful in other day-to -day related activities.

Classroom Implications of Transfer of Learning

1. The teacher should know that transfer of learning will not take place when both the old and new are unrelated. Hence, the teacher should endeavor to teach his/her subject-matter in a more meaningful and detailed way rather than by rote.

2. The teacher should provide the opportunity for his/her students to practice a subject-matter being discussed along with him/her.

When the learners are allowed to take active part in teaching learning activities, they will be able to repeat the task at another time.

3. For a transfer of learning to take place, the teacher should always emphasize the relationship that exists between one subject- matter and another.

4. The teacher should endeavor to develop positive attitudes towards a learning task so that the students can be motivated to like the task rather avoiding it.

5. It is believed that what students see, touch, feel or manipulate will be better remembered than the one they are not familiar with. Hence, for a meaningful transfer of learning to take place, the teacher should incorporate exercises that task the various senses of learners in the learning process.

Check Your Progress

1. List six ways of enhancing transfer of learning
2. Why do you consider Transfer of Learning a very important aspect in teaching?

3. Write short notes on:

i. Positive Transfer
ii. Negative Transfer
iii. Zero Transfer

Conclusion

The relevance of transfer of learning has been stressed in this unit. It will help the teachers on the action programmes that can facilitate learning transfer.

3. LET US SUM UP

In this unit we learnt about

- The meaning and concept of learning. The motive behind this is to ensure the learners have foundation knowledge of educational psychology and learning before actually advancing in other concepts.
- This unit helps us to understand characteristics, process of learning and Learning curve.
- The theories of Learning, the meaning of Instrumental/Operant Conditioning of B.F. Skinner. It mentioned the two major types of responses, the relevance of reinforcement as well as punishment to students' learning. Also, the implications of the theory to educational settings were discussed.
- Thorndike's theory emphasizes that the fundamental of learning is the association between sense impressions and impulses to action (stimuli and responses). The theory stresses readiness, exercises and effect as the conditions for learning.
- Classical conditioning theory was formulated by Ivan Pavlov and the basic tenet of the theory is that behavior of an organism can be manipulated using some environmental factors. The key relevance of theory to the learning is: it emphasizes practice of one task before moving on to another and encourages the use of motivation for effective learning.
- In this unit, we learnt about meaning of transfer of learning, theories of transfer of learning and classroom implications of transfer of learning

Unit End Exercises:

1. What is the relevance of Psychology to the learning process?
2. What is a learning curve? Describe a typical learning curve.
3. State any two causes of plateau.
4. Explain the educational importance of a learning curve. State the important characteristics of a learning curve.

5. Itemize and discuss main features of Operant Conditioning Theory.
6. What are the contributions of Skinner's Theory to educational process?
7. Describe Thorndike's law of readiness, exercises and effect. State the importance of these laws
8. What do you understand by Classical Conditioning Theory?
9. What are the implications of Classical Conditioning on the students' learning?
10. Write short notes on the following:

    a. Conditioned Stimulus
    b. Conditioned Response
    c. Unconditioned Response

11. What is transfer of learning
12. Discuss the three theories of transfer of learning
13. What are the implications of transfer of learning on pedagogical activities?

????

CHAPTER-6

FACTORS AFFECTING LEARNING

Unit Structure

0. Learning Objectives
1. Introduction
2. Maturation as factor in Learning
3. Attention and Perception as factor in Learning
4. Motivation as factor in Learning
5. Fatigue as factor in Learning
6. Let Us Sum Up
7. Suggested Readings

0. OBJECTIVES

After going through this unit, you will be able to ...

- Explain the factors affecting learning
- Explain how maturation affect learning
- Explain the concept and importance of attention and perception
- Explain the concept, principle, theories of motivation and technique of motivation students.
- Discuss Fatigue as factor in Learning

1. INTRODUCTION

Learning, as we know, can be considered as the process by which skills, attitudes, knowledge and concepts are acquired, understood, applied and extended. All human beings, engage in the process of learning, either consciously, sub-consciously or subliminally whether grownups or children. It is through learning that their competence and ability to function in their environment get enhanced. It is important to understand that while we learn some ideas and concepts through instruction or teaching, we also learn through our feelings and experiences. Feelings and experiences are a tangible part of our lives and these greatly influence what we learn, how we learn and why we learn.

Learning has been considered partly a cognitive process and partly a social and affective one. It qualifies as a cognitive process because it involves the functions of attention, perception, reasoning, analysis, drawing of conclusions, making interpretations and giving meaning to the observed phenomena. All of these are mental processes, which relate to the intellectual functions of the individual. Learning is a social and affective process, as the societal and cultural context in which we function and the feelings and experiences which we have, greatly influence our ideas, concepts, images and understanding of the world. These constitute inner subjective interpretations and represent our own unique, personalized constructions of the specific universe of functioning.

Our knowledge, ideas, concepts, attitudes, beliefs and the skills, which we acquire, are a consequence of these combined processes. The process of learning involves cognition, feeling, experience and a context. Individuals vary greatly with regard to their ability, capacity and interest in learning. You must have noticed such variations among your friends and students. In any family, children of the same parents differ with respect to what they can learn and how well they can learn.

For example, a particular child may be very good at acquiring practical skills such as repairing electrical gadgets, shopping for the household etc., while his brother or sister may in contrast be very poor on these, and good at academic tasks, instead. Even for yourself, you may be perplexed why you can do some tasks well, but not others given the same competence level.

For example, learning the tunes of songs and even their lyrics is often found to be easier than learning a formula or a poem. Do you ever wonder why this is so? You may have observed that for some people, learning driving, swimming, or cooking is achieved easily, while for some others it is a nightmare. Why this happens, what could be the underlying reasons, why individuals differ with respect to how, and what they learn, are the key questions addressed in the present unit. To find some answers to these questions, we will **try** to identify and understand the various factors affecting learning.

2. MATURATION AS FACTOR IN LEARNING

Maturation is an important factor that affects our learning is defined as "growth that proceeds regularly within a wide range of environmental conditions." Maturation is growth that takes place regularly in an individual without special condition of stimulation such as training and practice. Learning is possible only when a certain stage of maturation is also reached. Exercise and training

becomes fruitful only when a certain stage of maturation is attained. Maturation determines the readiness of the child for learning. Learning will be ineffective if the child has not attained the required level of maturity. There are individual differences in maturation. This means the rate of maturation varies with individuals. There are individual differences in the capacity to learn at the same age level. This is because of the difference of maturation level. Specific skills are learnt by children easily who mature earlier than others.

The 3R's i e reading, writing and reckoning can be learnt only after the maturation of muscular and brain capacities. Rate of learning ability is closely related to the maturation of the cerebral cortex. Deterioration of cortical tissues in old age brings about declination in the learning ability. So it can be said that learning is not independent of maturation, but must be based upon a sufficient stage of growth.

Learning is possible only when a certain stage of maturation is reached. However much we practice a six month old child with walking exercises, the infant cannot walk. The muscles have not matured enough for the infant to learn to walk. This particular learning is possible only when the nerves & the muscles have attained a particular stage of maturity & development.

Practice is most productive when properly articulated with maturational level. It is very essential for the teachers to know the maturational level of the pupils.

- Check Your Progress

1. Define maturation.

2. Fill up the blanks.

a. Learning is possible only when a certain stage ofis reached.
b. Maturation determines theof the child for learning.
c. Practice is most productive when properly articulated with

3. ATTENTION AND PERCEPTION AS FACTOR IN LEARNING

Another factor, which affects learning, is attention. Attention is always present in conscious life and is common to all types of mental activity. It is the characteristics of all conscious life. Every activity of yours is based on interest and attention. You can succeed in achieving your goals only when your attention is directed towards learning.

Attention is defined as the act of selective consciousness-**Ross Dumville** defined Attention as the concentration of consciousness upon one subject rather than another.

Characteristics of Attention

- Attention is focusing consciousness on one object. One object is the focus of attention. All other objects are in the margin of attention. (Right now, what is the focus of your attention? what objects are in the margin of your attention?)
- Attention is selective. We choose to attend to one object in preference to others.
- Attention is constantly shifting from focus to margin
- Attention is a state of preparedness where the muscles and sense organs ready themselves for attending
- Attention cannot be divided between two mental tasks.

Types of Attention

- **voluntary attention:**

a person actively searches out information that has personal relevance

- Selective attention:

a person selectively focuses attention on relevant information

- Involuntary attention:

a person is exposed to something surprising, novel, threatening, or unexpected

- **e.g.**: surprise, movement ,unusual sounds ,size of stimulus, contrast effects and color

Several factors affect attention. These are factors inherent in the object of attention

1. **Movement**: An animated picture elicits more attention than a still picture
2. **Size of an object**: Large letters attract more attention than tiny font.
3. **Contrast**: Dark letters stand out against a light background.
4. **Color**: Colors, especially bright ones, gain more attention than drab colors.
5. **Novelty**: A new gimmick in advertising is an instant hit
6. **Change in stimuli**: If the clock suddenly stops its ticking, it is likely to attract attention. If a teacher pauses in the midst of the lecture, the students are likely to pay more attention to the next few words
7. **Intensity**: A glaring light, sharp sound, fluorescent markers serve as attention grabbers.
8. **Repetition**: Words of a song that are repeated or words in a lecture that are repeated attract attention.

Significance of Attention

It is basic need for all types of learning. Every moment of yours is attracted by many stimuli of the environment. Your mind is not able to concentrate on all the stimuli at the same time. It is because of attention that you are able to concentrate on important aspect of a single object.

Consider a classroom, where there are lot of things like, desk, bench, chalk, black board, duster, fan and charts. When a teacher shows you a particular chart, you pay attention to that. It shifts the focus of learner to the chart this helps them to learn more about it.

Therefore, it can be said that attention helps you to clear the vivid objects.

- It arouses interest in learners to learn a particular thing.
- It increases efficiency of the learner
- It motivates learners to learn more
- It make the learners ready to learn
- It brings a state of alternates in learners for doing task
- It helps the learner to perceive events or ideas.

Thus, attention is a necessary condition for any task in the classroom. It is the hub of entire learning process. It is essential for learning as well as understanding well. Attention is an essential factor for teachers as well as students. If you are attentive in classroom, you are fully prepared to receive any stimulus. It enables you to learn properly within a period. It helps you to achieve the target within short period and with reasonable amount of effort.

- Check Your Progress

1. What do you mean by attention? State the characteristic of attention.
2. State two significance of attention

PERCEPTION

Perception is the process through which a person is exposed to information, attends to the information, and comprehends the information.

Exposure: a person receives information through his/her senses **Attention:** a person allocates processing capacity to a stimulus **Comprehension:** a person interprets the information to obtain meaning from it

Meaning: Perception is the mental process by which you get knowledge of external world. You receive innumerable impression through the sense organs. You select some of these and organise them into unit, which convey some meaning. The transformation of sensation into organised pattern is called as perception.

Perception = sensation + Meaning

For E.g. Eyes react to light and give us the knowledge of brightness, nose reacts to smell and give us the knowledge of pleasant or unpleasant smell, ear react to the sound of barking and gives us the knowledge of presence of a dog.

Perception is an active state of mind in which it reacts on sensation and interprets it. The basis of perception is sensation.

Importance of Perception in Learning

Learning depends on an individual's precepts. If you are able to perceive a thing correctly then right learning will take place. Learning will proceed in a proper direction due to correct precepts. Both sensation and perception play an important role in you learning. Sensations are the first impression so it has to be absolutely clear. Sensations give rise to perception and on that basis you get a proper understanding of an object, idea or an experience. Learning depends upon accurate and efficient perception and perception depends upon the sensation, which depends on the normal functioning of the sense organs. Thus perception is important for proper learning and understanding.

Check Your Progress

1. Explain, what do you mean by perception?
2. Discuss the importance of perception in classroom teaching and learning process.

6.4. MOTIVATION AS FACTOR IN LEARNING

The knowledge of how to stimulate the students to participate meaningfully in classroom will go a long way in assisting the teachers. This unit therefore provides the learners the opportunity to understand different theories of motivation and how to apply these theories to their day-to-day classroom teaching/learning activities.

Motivation is defined as an inspiration that propels someone into an action. It is an internal state or condition that activates and gives direction to our thoughts, feelings, and actions (Lahey, 1995). In the opinion of Oladele (1998), motivation is a process by which the learner's internal energies are directed toward various goal objects in his/her environment. These energies or arousals push an individual in achieving his goals. An individual may be highly motivated to perform well in a task and completely unmotivated in another. This means that when people are motivated, they will work tirelessly to achieve their aspirations.

Maslow (1970) believed that motivation leads to growth and development, and that need satisfaction is the most important sole factor underlying motivation. Maslow furthered explained that man is perpetually in needs and that the resources to satisfy those needs are limited. In view of this, man places his/her wants on the scale of preference, that he/she selects the most pressing need. After this need has been satisfied, it becomes less important, paving way for the next on the rank.

The needs of man may either be primary or secondary. Primary needs are the physiological wants of man. It may be the need for water, rest, sexual intercourse, hunger and thirst. Secondary needs are the desire for autonomy, affection, or the need for safety and security. For example, the desire of a labourer to take a glass of water after thirst is a primary need. At the same time, craving of the students to stay in a serene classroom environment is a secondary need.

Types of Motivation

There are two types of motivation or arousals. They can either be internally or externally driven. The desire for food or sex arises from within us (intrinsic), while the yearning to obtain recognition or approval is influenced by the conditions in our environment (extrinsic). In view of the above explanation, motivation is divided into intrinsic and extrinsic.

1. **Intrinsic Motivation:** Is an internal force or motive within the individual which propels him/her into emitting certain behavior. It is an innate or genetically predetermined disposition to behave in a particular way when he/she faces a particular situation. This type of motivation can make an individual to have the feelings of self- confidence and competence (Deci and Ryan, 1985). A student who is intrinsically motivated may carry out a task because of the enjoyment he/she derives from such a task. In another way, a dog that sees a bone and runs for it, did that because of the satisfaction it derives from eating bone. This type of behavior does not require any prior learning. Sighting the bone changes the behavior of the dog and propels it to act.

2. **Extrinsic Motivation:** Is the external or environmental factor, which sets the individual's behavior into motion. The incentive/ reinforcer drives an individual's behavior towards a goal. A student that is extrinsically motivated will execute an action in order to obtain some reward or avoid some sanctions. For example, a student who read hard for the examination did so because of the desire to obtain better grade. The case also goes for a runner who wants to win a prize, he/she will need constant practice than a person who wants to run for the fun of it. Extrinsic rewards should be used with caution because they have the

potential for decreasing exiting intrinsic motivation.

For example extrinsic incentive may spur a student to actively participate in the task for which the student has no interest, but may undermine intrinsic and continuing motivation in him/her (Deci et al, 1985). Therefore, students' motivation automatically has to do with the students' desire to participate in the learning process. It also concerns the reasons or goals that underlie their involvement or non-involvement in academic activities.

Theories of Motivation

Different psychologists have developed several theories on motivation. Notable among them are discuss as follows

Maslow's Theory of Motivation

Abraham Maslow was a foremost Psychologist. He developed a theory (Human Needs) in which he identified seven vital human needs according to level of urgency or exigency. These needs according to the Maslow are:

1. **Physiological Needs:** These are the biological or survival needs of man. They are the most basic needs that control the other needs. Until these needs are fulfilled or satisfied, man will not be able to go to the next level. Examples of these needs are the desire to eat food when hungry, drink water when thirsty or the need for rest, sex, air or to excrete unwanted materials from the body systems. After these survivals needs have been adequately taken care, they become less important and one moves to the next which is the desire for security and safety.

2. **Safety and Security Needs:** Human beings require safety and protection from danger or external aggressors. After one has successfully dealt with physiological needs, it is desirable to cater for psychological needs. At this point, Man will be thinking of where to live and efforts will be made to keep him/her from impending dangers, threats or hazards. The hallmark of these needs is the quest by an individual to seek for conducive or peaceful abode. For example, the desire of war victims to migrate from their original country to become refugees in another country is the need for safety and security. Also, a chicken that quickly hibernates under its mother on sighting an eagle did so because of its desire for safety.

3. **Love and Belongingness Needs:** This involves the aspiration of man to establish a cordial relationship with others. It is the need of man to love and be loved. At this level of need, people will like to extend their hands of fellowship or comradeship to their friends, mates, co-workers or neighbors. They equally will expect that such gestures be reciprocated by others. Onyehalu (1988) believes that this need is manifested in our affiliations and friendships.

4. **Achievement Needs:** Achievement needs are divided into two. These are the need to achieve success and the need to avoid failure or setback. The need to attain success or freedom drives man to go extra miles. This need motivates an individual to emit a behavior that will make him/her command respect from others.

5. **Self-Esteem Needs:** These are the things we desire in order that our ego will be boosted. After the individual has been accorded respect or recognition by others, the next thing for him/her is to start seeking for the things that will make him/her enjoy considerable influence from others. The ability of someone to fulfill this condition makes him/her feel superior and self-confident. Inability to fulfill this need, makes a person feel dejected or inferior.

6. **Aesthetic Needs:** These needs include the desire of people to pursue or admire beautiful things; their desire for beautiful and expensive cars, houses, materials, gorgeous and expensive dresses and beautiful surroundings with well-trimmed and maintained flowers.

7. **Self-Actualization Needs:** When a person has successfully achieved or gained the most basic needs or wants, then such an individual will want to get a rare opportunity. It is the time when a person will like to distinguish him/herself, by seeking for power or extra-ordinary achievement. At this point person is said to have reached the peak of his potentials.

Henry Murray's Theory of Motivation

Murray like Maslow also propounded the theory of motivation. He divided his theory into two, viscerogenic and psychogenic needs.

1. **Viscerogenic Needs:** These are referred to as biological or physiological needs. They are the primary needs and these include the desire for water, sex, sleep, food, air and excretion of waste products. They are the higher order needs.

2. **Psychogenic Needs:** These needs correspond with other needs in Maslow's theory. They are secondary needs. Examples of these are the longing for safety and security, love and comradeship, self- esteem, beautiful things or serene environment, rare or dominant positions etc.

Classroom Implications of Theory of Motivation

- It is important for the teacher to know the basic needs of his/her students and cater for these according to level of their important. For example, the teacher needs to think first of students' food, rest or health before thinking of teaching them.
- When the teacher praises his/her students for doing well in their study or assignment, they will be spurred to sustain that effort.

- A classroom, which is well decorated or adorned with beautiful charts, and learning materials will be students' friendly. The students' minds will always be attracted to the activities in a beautifully adorned classroom.
- In the classroom, students like being recognized or respected. When their views are recognized or respected, they will have their confidence boosted and developed.
- From the beginning of the lesson, the teacher should endeavour to make his/her students know possible outcome of the lesson. It is when the students know what they are likely to achieve from the lesson that their attention will be arrested and sustained.
- Feedback is necessary if the interest of the students must be sustained in the classroom. So the teacher should always strive to let them know how they are performing in the teaching- learning activities.
- The teacher should also provide/plan for extra-curricular activities for his/her students. When the teacher does this, the students will have opportunity of establishing a genuine interaction among them. Besides, they will be able to display their hidden talents.
- When dealing with the students in the classroom, the teacher should take into consideration, the developmental changes and differences in the students before deciding on the particular motivation pattern to be employed.

Check Your Progress

1. What problems are associated with the use of extrinsic reward?
2. How does learning objectives affect student motivation?
3. How can you promote intrinsic motivation in student?
4. Write short notes on the following:

   i. Physiological Needs
   ii. Viscerogenic Needs

iv. Aesthetic Needs

5. FATIGUE AS FACTOR OF LEARNING

It is quite essential to do away with fatigue in the process of learning as fatigue becomes an obstacle in the task to be performed or at least reduces its rate of progress. The truth of the matter is that the proportion in which the students becomes fatigued, his achievement curve shows a downward trend. Achievement decreases with the increase in fatigue. Hence, educational psychology makes a detailed study of the cause of fatigue and of the methods of alleviating it.

What is Fatigue?

Fatigue is the state of reduced interest and desire, and this constitutes psychological explanation. It is the state or condition in which the nerves do not react and mind becomes lax and inert. Evidently, fatigue is neither purely physical nor exclusively mental. It is a psychological state of exhaustion. Reduce efficiency or capacity of body as well as mind is implicit in this phenomenon.

Kinds of Fatigue

Fatigue is of many kinds just as capacity. However, it is generally believed to be of four kinds.

1. **Mental Fatigue:** Mental work or any kind of strain on the mind reduces the capacity of th e mind for work and causes mental fatigue. Thus in mental fatigue, the mind tries or the capacity to its minute fibers for work is diminished.
2. **Physical Fatigue:** This type of fatigue results in the reduction in the capacity of the muscles of the body and a feeling of fatigue. In this way physical fatigue is brought about by physical exertion. Even though the body feels tired due to mental exertion which should normally result in mental fatigue, yet on account of close relation of the two, it also produces physical fatigue. Thus mental fatigue is unavoidable and it lead to physical fatigue.
3. **Nervous Fatigue:** The subconscious mind of man is extremely active and since in the process of its work it consumes energy, in due course of time it naturally produces a feeling of fatigue and depression. Nervous fatigue can also result in the subconscious is extremely tired due to mental conflict.
4. **Boredom:** Boredom and fatigue are not identical. Fatigue is the result of the use of energy but boredom is the feeling of tiredness due to an incomplete or improper expulsion of energy.

5. If you go to a friend and he is busy in some work you become bored. Similarly, you get bored if a person persists in talking about the same thing day after. Boredom result in restlessness, a state induced by our inability to find proper use for our capacity for work.

Ways of Removing Fatigue

1. Sleep: Getting proper 8 hrs of sleep is necessary.

2. Relaxation: sitting or lying in a relaxed position, doing activities which are favourites also eliminate fatigue.
3. Balance of work and rest
4. Change in the nature of work
5. Recreation
6. Change in Emotions

Reducing Fatigue in School and classroom

The following points can be kept in the view to fight fatigue in the classroom situation.

1. **Satisfactory physical condition:** the school and the classroom should be attractive and clean. The furniture must be quite comfortable.

2. **Medical Check Up:** Sick children are soon tired. Sometimes some children are healthy apparently but they may be suffering from some chronic ailments. They cannot carry on sustained activity for a long time. Weak eye-sight exhaust the individual very soon.

3. **Mid-day Meals:** Hungry stomachs invite fatigue during activity. Therefore, children should be provide with mid-day meals or other light refreshments in the school time.

4. **Supply of fresh air:** The rooms must be well ventilated for fresh air and light. Oxygen is a necessary thing to fight fatigue. There should be enough outdoor activities also.

5. **Motivation:** the lesson must be made quite interesting. Therefore, various teaching techniques should be implemented during teaching-learning process.

6. **Co-curricular activities:** Extracurricular activities prove very refreshing, interesting and instructive to the children. Therefore, there should be ample provisions of such activities in the school.

Check Your Progress

1. What do you mean by Fatigue? Explain the kinds of fatigue
2. Explain the ways of removing the fatigue school and classroom situation.

6. LETS SUM UP

This unit has prepared the teachers to focus on the factors that affect the learning process.

- We discussed how maturation contribute to the learning
- The various strategies teachers can employ to keep the attention and give clear perception of the students in the teaching-learning activities.
- We discussed the Definitions, Types and Theories of motivation which has given an understanding how to motivate the student in classroom.
- Fatigue is an important factor that influences the learning process; we focused on removes the aspects which create fatigue in order to have effective learning.

Unit End Exercises:

1. Explain how maturation affects the teaching learning process in classroom.
2. Discuss the significance of attention and perception to learning.
3. Define motivation. Differentiate between intrinsic and extrinsic motivation
4. Distinguish between Maslow and Murray theories of motivation
5. What is the relevance of motivation to students learning?
6. Discuss the kind of fatigue, how as a teacher we can remove the fatigue of students in classroom situation.

????

CHAPTER-7

MENTAL PROCESSES RELATED TO LEARNING

Unit structure:

0. Objectives
1. Introduction
2. Thinking

1. Concept of Thinking
2. Tools of Thinking
3. Types of Thinking

0. OBJECTIVES

After going through this unit, you will able to

- To develop an understanding of the mental processes related to learning.
- To develop an understanding of the nature and concept of thinking.
- To acquaint the learners with the different types of thinking.

1. INTRODUCTION

Psychology deals with the study of the mental processes which includes how people think, perceive, remember and learn. Thus, it is concerned with internal processes such as thinking, memory, imagination, reasoning etc. Thought or capacity to think was at one time held to be not only the most distinctive characteristic of human nature but also the one which most clearly distinguished the human being from other creatures.

The great philosopher Descartes had said, "I think, so I exist", implying that thought is the very essence of human existence. Thinking, therefore, represents the most complex psychological processes. Most of the things in the world produced by man are products of his thinking and reasoning abilities. Even to understand, appreciate or use the things developed by man, one has to employ the powers of thinking and reasoning. Thus, powers of thinking and reasoning may be considered to be essential tools for the welfare and meaningful existence of the individual as well as the society.

Learning not only involves thinking processes but also retaining or storing the acquired material and also retrieving and remembering the related material. It is a known fact that we neither retain nor remember everything that has been learnt or experienced. This phenomenon of losing is evidenced by our inability to remember what we have learnt and is known as forgetting.

Thus, in this unit we will try to learn something about thinking, reasoning, memory and forgetting, which is an integral part of human behavior.

2. THINKING

1. Concept of Thinking:

Thinking is a complex process which involves manipulation of information as we form concepts. It also engages in problem solving, reasoning and making decisions. Thinking is a higher cognitive function and the analysis of thinking processes is part of cognitive psychology. Thinking is a pattern of behavior in which we make use of internal representations (symbols, signs etc.) of things and events for the solution of some specific, purposeful problem.

Definitions:

Ross: Thinking is a mental activity in its cognitive aspect. Kolesnik: Thinking is the reorganization of concepts.

Woodworth: Thinking is mental exploration for finding out the solution of a problem.

Characteristics:

- It is one of the most important aspects of ones cognitive behavior.
- It depends on both – perception and memory.
- Thinking is a mental process which starts with a problem and concludes with its solution.
- It involves trial and error; analysis and synthesis; foresight and hindsight.
- It is a symbolic behavior.
- It is a cognitive activity.
- It is always directed to achieve some purpose.
- It is different from day-dreaming and imagination.
- It is a problem-solving behavior.
- There is mental exploration instead of motor exploration...

(e.g.: if a person gets locked in a room and loses his keys and he starts searching for them in different places then this becomes motor exploration; but if he tries to think of different ways of how he can get out of the room then this becomes mental exploration- THINKING.)

- Thinking is a symbolic activity. (e.g.: engineers use mental images and symbols to design the plan for buildings)

Check your Progress

1. What do you understand by thinking?
2. Enumerate the characteristics of thinking.

2. Tools of Thinking:

1. Percepts, 2. Images / Object, 3. Concepts, 4. Symbols and Signs, 5. Language.

1. **Percepts:** A mental impression of something perceived by the senses, viewed as the basic component in the formation of concepts is called percepts. Percepts are recognition and interpretation of sensory stimuli based chiefly on memory. Thus, the percept is a perceived form of external stimuli. The percept also binds sensations from all of the senses in a whole.

2. **Images / Objects:** Often images are used as an instrument of thinking. These images may be images of personal experiences of objects, persons or scenes actually seen, heard or felt. These mental pictures symbolize actual objects, experiences and activities.
3. **Concepts:** A concept is a 'general idea' that stands for a general class and represents the common characteristic of all objects or events of this general class. The concept formation saves our efforts in thinking. E.g. 'Man is mortal'; you do not perceive a particular man but mankind in general i.e. including women. Thus the generalized 'man' is a concept.

4. **Symbols & signs:** These represent & stand for a substitute for actual subjects, experiences and activities. e.g. Traffic lights, railway signals, school bells, songs, slogans etc stand for symbolic expression. Thus symbols and signs stimulate & economize thinking. They tell us at once what to do or how to act.

5. **Language:** It serves not only as a link for intercommunication but also acts as a tool for thinking. It consists of words therefore uses symbols; sometimes we use gestures in our language. When one is listening, reading or writing, one is stimulated to think. Language is a most effective & developed tool for the process of thinking.

Check your Progress

1. Enlist the tools of thinking.
2. Explain the tools of thinking with appropriate examples.

3. Types of Thinking

a. Convergent Thinking
b. Divergent Thinking
c. Critical Thinking
d. Reflective Thinking
e. Lateral Thinking

a. Convergent Thinking

Convergent thinking proceeds on the assumption that there is one single best solution to any problem, and also that the solution can be arrived at on the basis of the existing knowledge. Thus, convergent thinking involves the direction of all thought process in one single direction. "Convergent" thinking is in which the person is good at bringing material from a variety of sources to bear on a problem, in such a way as to produce the "correct" answer. Because of the need for consistency and reliability, this is really the only form of thinking which standardized intelligence tests (and even national exams) can test.

b. Divergent Thinking

"Divergent" thinking may start from existing knowledge, but it proceeds in different directions and are not limited or bound by existing knowledge. At times divergent thinker may question and doubt the adequacy of the existing knowledge. This type of thinking may start from a common point and move outward into a variety of perspectives. When fostering divergent thinking, teachers use the content as a vehicle to prompt diverse or unique thinking among students rather than a common view. Divergent thinking is also creative thinking. It generates something new or different. It involves having a different idea that works as well or better than previous ideas. Thus, divergent thinkers have an open mind. He is not controlled by the belief that there is "one best solution" to any problem or "the correct answer" to any question.

Basically divergent thinking is a mode in which a person or group makes themselves open to new ideas. Generally speaking, they are working with, what we might call, an open ended problem, a problem for which there is, there may be, many creative possible solutions, so the divergent thinking process is one in which we are open to all those ideas and we generate lots of new ideas. The difference between the two can be seen in the following table:

Convergent Thinking

Divergent Thinking

Non creative people have convergent thinking.

Creative people have divergent thinking.

Produces single correct answer.

Produces variety of responses.

It is stimulus bound.

It is stimulus free.

The problem is solved by known or common method.

The problem is solved by different innovative methods.

It is rigid, stereotyped & mechanically operated.

It is novel, exploratory & venturesome.

It is measured by intelligence test which includes remembering, recognition & manipulation of some concrete material.

It is measured by creativity tests in which novelty, flexibility & originality are given more weightage.

It is known as Reasoning or Rational Thinking.

It is known as Creative Thinking, Imaginative or Original Thinking.

c. Critical thinking

Critical thinking assesses the worth and validity of something existent. It involves precise, persistent, objective analysis. When teachers try to get several learners to think convergent, they try to help them develop common understanding.

Norris, Stephen P:"Critical thinking is deciding rationally what to or what not to believe."

According to Moore and Parker, Critical Thinking is "the careful, deliberate determination of whether we should accept, reject, or suspend judgment about a claim, and the degree of confidence with which we accept or reject it.

"Broadly speaking, critical thinking is concerned with reason, intellectual honesty, and open-mindedness, as opposed to emotionalism, intellectual laziness, and closed-mindedness."

Attributes of a critical thinker:

- asks pertinent questions
- assesses statements and arguments
- is able to admit a lack of understanding or information

- has a sense of curiosity
- is interested in finding new solutions
- is able to clearly define a set of criteria for analyzing ideas
- is willing to examine beliefs, assumptions, and opinions and weigh them against facts
- listens carefully to others and is able to give feedback
- sees that critical thinking is a lifelong process of self- assessment
- suspends judgment until all facts have been gathered and considered
- looks for evidence to support assumption and beliefs
- is able to adjust opinions when new facts are found
- looks for proof
- examines problems closely
- Is able to reject information that is incorrect or irrelevant.

d. Reflective thinking

Dewey's definition of reflective thinking:

"Active, persistent, and careful consideration of any belief or supposed form of knowledge in the light of the grounds that support it and the further conclusion to which it tends"

Reflective thinking is normally a slow process. It takes considerable time to work on inferring and combining by reflecting upon what we have learnt:

This is a higher form of thinking.

- It aims at solving complex problems.
- It requires reorganization of all the relevant experiences and the finding of new ways of reacting to a situation or of removing an obstacle instead of a simple association of experiences or ideas.
- There is insightful cognitive approach in reflective thinking.
- It takes all the relevant facts arranged in a logical order into account in order to arrive at a solution of the problem in hand.
- It links the information we possess into tighter network, thus helps to remember the matter better.
- It criticizes what one has learned and tries to expose weaknesses and shortcomings.
- Enhancing decision making requires that we learn from our successes and failures and catalog mentally for future retrieval

what has occurred and why.

e. Lateral thinking

Lateral thinking is a term coined by Edward de Bono, a Maltese psychologist, physician and writer. It first appeared in the title of his book The Use of Lateral Thinking, published in 1967. De Bono defines lateral thinking as methods of thinking concerned with changing concepts and perception. Lateral thinking is about reasoning that is not immediately obvious and about ideas that may not be obtainable by using only traditional step-by-step logic.

De Bono identifies four critical factors associated with lateral thinking: (1) recognize dominant ideas that polarize perception of a problem, (2) searching for different ways of looking at things, (3) relaxation of rigid control of thinking, and (4) use of chance to encourage other ideas.

Lateral thinking involves discarding the obvious, leavingbehind traditional modes of thought, and throwing awaypreconceptions.

- Explanation: A person would use lateral thinking when they want to move from one known idea to creating new ideas.
- Lateral thinking can be used to help in solving problems but can also be used for much more.
- With lateral thinking problems can be solved and questions can be answered, as lateral thinkers are able to use their creative

skills to change perceptions and come up with new concepts and ideas.

- The lateral thinking technique of 'challenge' is designed to prevent the mind sliding smoothly down the existing patterns.
- Lateral Thinking is the ability to add a slight "twist" to the pattern of logical thinking to produce an unexpected answer!
- Essentially, lateral thinking is a way of attacking problems from other angles, as opposed to the more traditional linear and logical ways. De bono uses the example of chess, where logic normally suffices, if the pieces are a given. Lateral thinking acknowledges that in real life we mostly just assume the pieces are given, when really we need to change those pieces or look beyond them for the most useful solutions.

Lateral Thinking helps individual to develop skills to: Increase productive idea output.

Design the future.

Find fresh new solutions to intractable problems. Escape the constraints of routine thinking.

Appreciate the diversity of thinking among team members. Plan and lead innovation meetings that deliver powerful results. Find new areas of opportunity.

Unit End Exercises:

1. Which are the different types of thinking?
2. Differentiate between convergent and divergent thinking.
3. What do you understand by critical thinking?

????

CHAPTER-8

MEMORY

Unit Structure:

0. Objective
1. Memory
2. Forgetting
3. Imagination
4. Reasoning
5. Let us sum up
6. Glossary
7. Suggested reading

0. OBJECTIVES

After going through this unit, you will able to:

- To gain an insight into the mental processes involving memory, forgetting, imagination and reasoning.

1. MEMORY

It is said education is a life long process and we are learning all the time. But simply learning without being able to repeat that in another situation or occasion is of no use. Thus we must be able to make use of past experiences. We must be able to reproduce it. This power of reproduction is known as memory, or the ability to retain and recall the past events to present consciousness. This implies that memory is the reproduction of past experience even without the presence of the stimulus.

Guilford: "Memory is the retention or storage of information in any form".

Woodworth & Marquis: "Memory consists in learning what was previously learned".

Ryburn: "The power that we have to store our experience and to bring them back into the field of consciousness some time after the experience have occurred is termed as memory".

F'iedsetal: "Memory is the ability to retain & reproduce impressions once perceived"

Memory is the special ability of our mind to store when we learn something to recollect &reproduce it after some time. Memory is the complex process involving learning, retention, recall & recognition. The experiences which we undergo, leaves traces in our minds in the form of 'Schemas'. The length of our retention depends on the strength & quality of the traces.

Types of Memory:

1. **Immediate Memory**: This is also known as short term memory. This memory is when the individual has to reproduce immediately after he has learnt something, thus the time span is very less for the matter to be registered in the consciousness. Hence the learnt matter is forgotten rapidly. e.g. we may first look at the seat number of our ticket & once we sit down we forget about it. In this type of memory, the retention time is very brief. Immediate memory is needed which helps

us to learn a thing immediately with speed and accuracy, remember it for a short duration and forget it rapidly after use.

2. **Short-term memory:** This type of memory is also called as temporary memory. It is not short lived as the immediate memory. The information temporarily stored in short-term memory may last as long as thirty seconds even if the material is not being rehearsed. However, some people are able to retain much more information in short- term memories by a process called chunking, which groups information by coding it, e.g. the number 143254376 can be remembered by listing under three heads: 143, 254, 376 for better remembering.

3. **Long term memory:** This is also known as Permanent Memory. Here the individual learns and retains the information for a very long period of time. There is an interval of time between learning & recall or reproduction. Thus permanent memory is involved

e.g. knowing our account number of the bank or the phone number.

So we see that memory is a process involving learning & reproduction. The amount of material that can be immediately reproduced after one repetition is called **span of memory.** The phenomenon of memory may be studied under four different aspects: viz.the four R's.

1. Registration or Learning
2. Retention
3. Recall
4. Recognition

1. <u>REGISTRATION OR LEARNING</u>: Before remembering it must be registered or learnt. Learning requires time. It has economical use of time in learning. The most efficient methods of learning or memorizing that would yield the best results from the point of view of remembering effectively for a long time are as follows:

A. **Rote Memorization:** This is learning without understanding. Yet meaningful material is easily learnt than non-sense material. It's easy to learn poetry than prose; prose is easy to learn than disconnected words. Disconnected words are easy to learn than nonsense words. Thus logical sequence is important, along with the systematic arrangement of ideas. However, mechanical learning must be avoided as it is less effective.

B. **Spaced V/S Mass Learning:** In spaced learning, the learner has been allowed some rest in memorization. The subject is not required to memorize the assignment in one continuous time period. Intervals are provided. The principle of 'work & rest' is followed. In mass learning, the subject has to memorize the assigned material at one sitting without any interval or rest, until it is mastered. Shorter study periods are better for young pupils & slow learners. Spaced learning benefits pupils of lower classes, when motivation level is low or material is complex & difficult to understand. It is better to introduce periods of rest while studying. This helps in removing the monotony of long periods of study. Attention also does not flag and fatigue is avoided. Mass learning is effective when the pupils are very intelligent or are highly motivated. Although, both the methods of learning are found to be useful and effective in one situation or the other. In fact, success in the use of a particular method depends more on the abilities of the individual and the nature and range of the material to be memorized than on the method itself.

C. **Whole verses Part method of learning:** Let's take the example of a poem, when the poem is read again & again from start to finish; this is whole method of learning. This method can be adopted when the material is not very lengthy & when the material is logically arranged. Less time is used compared to part method. Here again the poem for example is broken down to parts or stanzas & then learnt, thus slow learners & average students are benefitted . The learner is motivated each time he masters the parts, thus the whole content is slowly mastered.

Even when the material is large & is not well organized, this method can be used.

D. **Recitation:** The best method of learning where by the student reads the lesson few times & then reviews the lesson without the book i.e. he recites the material learnt to him. Studies have shown that self-recitation is better & time saving than just reading & rereading because permanent retention is achieved. Learner is able to detect his weakness & rectify them thus he knows his progress as well.

E. **Mnemonic Devices:** Grouping always helps to memorize easily, thus we learn poetry easily compared to prose, but many material come without such natural grouping. Thus artificial associations are made to associate the ideas or the material. Thus memory which is improved by use of artificial associates is called Mnemonics. Thus things are learnt verbatim without understanding it .e.g. VIBGYOR whose letters represent the colors of the rainbow.

2. **RETENTION:**The process of learning involves the stage of retention thus learning becomes permanent. 'Retention is the inactive state of learnt activity'. The learning activity leaves a mark on the brain structure. This mark is called a 'Memory Trace' which is imprinted on the Cerebral Cortex. This preservation of the memory trace in the brain is retaining of the learning activity. This can be compared to the traces or marks in the sand e.g. our footprints made on the sand. The deeper the trace, the longer the retention, the weak traces slowly fades away.

Memory can be improved, but the depth of the trace or retention is difficult to improve by practice the reason being the traces that are made, depend on the genetic inheritance.

Retention however can be measured in three ways

a) Recall b) Recognition & c) Relearning.

a. **Recall Method:** A direct method of testing retention, where the capacity to recall & reproduce is tested. We can recall matter, only if we have retained it. e.g. in a writing a test: the pupil's retention & recall is tested. But sometimes we are not able to recall, even when we know the matter. So we cannot measure the retention. Therefore this is the poorest retention score of all that is learnt.

b. **Recognition Method:** This method is widely used now. A response given from which the pupil has to pick out the correct answer or recognize the correct answer. This ability of

recognizing the correct answer helps measure the power of retention. This has a higher score of testing retention than recall method & also puts less strain on the child e.g. multiple choice questions, or questions based on a picture or map.

c. **Relearning Method:** Let's give an example ABC is learning a long poem & it takes him 20 minutes & 4 trials to memorize it. After a few days ABC again learns the poem & now in 10 minutes & two trials he learns it fully. Thus we can assume that retention has taken place because the time & the number of trials have reduced. Thus this method is the best compared to recognition & recall methods.

3. **RECALL**- The third aspect of memory is recall. We learn because we need to recall them at some point of time or other. So we can say that recall is the mental revival of past experiences. The least index of retention because we are unable to

remember even though we know it. Recall depends on the mental condition & the memory trace formed.

4. **RECOGNITION**– Recall & recognition are closely related. Recall provides the material in memory, while recognition is the process of accepting or rejecting. Recognition is better than recall as an index of retention. Recognition starts with the object given whereas recalls find the object from the mind. Thus, when we meet a person, recognize that person's face, but may not be able to recall his name. Recognition is more a passive behavior than an active process like recall.

Recall

Recognition

1) Recall is the revival of the past the experiences.

1) Recognition is the perception & identification of an object

2) The process begins in the mind.

2) The process begins from the object

3) It involves active mental process

3) It involves passive mental process

4) Least index of measuring retention.

4) High index of measuring retention.

e.g. short answer type questions involves recall

e.g. Multiple choice questions, sees the picture & recognize the answer.

Check your progress.

1. Explain the components of memory.
2. What are the different types of memories?
3. Enumerate with examples, the different ways in the process of memorizing.
4. What are the different ways of measuring recall?
5. Differentiate between recall and recognition.

2. FORGETTING

In our daily life we have experienced the time we want to recall the name of a friend and we realize that we have forgotten it. Forgetting occurs only when some learning has taken place. If there is no learning then there is no forgetting. Thus forgetting & remembering are two sides of the same coin.

So when we are unable to remember it's called forgetting.

Munn: "Forgetting is the loss permanent or temporary of the ability to recall or recognize something learnt earlier"

Drever: "Forgetting means failure at any time to recall an experience, when attempting to do so or perform an action previously done.

Bhatia: "Forgetting is the failure of an individual to review in consciousness an idea or a group of ideas without the help of original stimulus."

Thus forgetting is being unable to find the correct information. (from the mind) at the given situation. Forgetting is temporary at times when later we can remember the names & actions whereas forgetting is said to be permanent when in no situation we are able to recall the information.

Let's see why we are unable to recall information & Why do we forget?

Factors influencing Forgetting:-

1. **Decay through disuse or Theory of Decay:**

Forgetting is a process of fading of the learnt matter with passage of time. According to this view, the vivid impressions created in the cerebral cortex fade away as time passes. Such fading or decay could be the result of the normal metabolic processes of the brain. As time passes, these processes might cause the traces of material once learned to disintegrate gradually and eventually to disappear altogether.

2. Interference of Association or Theory of interference:

Here we see that forgetting is not caused just by fading away of traces, but by influence of the intervening activities.

a. **Retroactive interferences**: Here new learning works backward & interferes with old learning.
b. **Proactive Inhibition** or Interference: Here what we have learnt previously interferes with the new learning. Forgetting in our daily life is more due to proactive interference; our ability to recall what we have learnt is reduced by experiences previously learnt.

3. Theory of Repression or motivated forgetting

The two earlier theories are physiological process of affecting mental trace or interference in learning. But here the person is not given importance. For some people, forgetting is a psychological process, where by will the unpleasant or conflicting experiences are repressed & pushed into the unconscious & forgotten. Thus repression is done because it may cause anxiety to remember the experiences e.g. remembering loved ones whom we will never see again, we want to forget those people who hurt us.

4. **Emotions:** Rise in emotions like fear or anger or love lead to forget the learned experiences e.g. a student afraid of a teacher may forget what has been learnt.

5. **Change of stimulus conditions:** we may have learnt in a specific environment, but we forget in the changed environment

e.g. we can say the speech well at home but in front of the audience, we are unable to speak.

6. **Poor Health:** this prevents us from remembering learnt material.

7. **Defective mental state**, fatigue, lack of interest or willingness all lead to forgetting

Factors which helps to minimizing Forgetting or Factors whichhelp to improve Memory

1. Rate of Learning: It's a fallacy that rapid learning is associated with rapid forgetting 'easy come easy do'. But the reverse is actually true, in rapid learning forgetting is slow & when learning is slow forgetting is rapid. Thus a slow learner, would eventually lose interest in the subject thus forget the material rather quickly than a quick learner.

2. Over learning: forgetting is said to be taking place as soon as we stop learning. So we must recall immediately after we have learnt & it must continue after intervals. Learning must be carried beyond the point where recall is just barely possible. Overlearning , beyond the point of complete mastery, strengthens the impressions in the brain.
3. Periodic review: this is very similar to self recitation thus as soon as we learn we start the review of the data. Reviews at frequent intervals prevent the decay of the learnt data or information.

4. Kind of Material: easy, simple, meaningful and logically related materials are easy to retain & forgotten less rapidly. Thus general concepts, scientific interpretations are better retained. Meaningless materials are forgotten quickly. Thus associations make material meaningful & quick to remember.

5. Intention to Learn: firm determination or strong will to learn is required to achieve success. Same material given to sets of students wherein one is willing & other is not unwilling, in such cases we see that retention was greater in those students who had a determination to learn.

6. Proper Methods of Learning: economical method must be chosen depending on the material to be learnt, so we chose spaced versus mass or whole versus part learning.

7. Self recitation: After reading a lesson a few times, the student must try to review the whole thing without the help of a book. This method may also be termed as attempted recall and it makes a more economical use of one's study time. It also helps towards permanent retention.

How can we improve the way we learn?:

1. **A will to learn:** Learning is better achieved when there is a drive to learn. Thus without intention learning is not achieved much.
2. **Use Multiple sensory learning:** Things are better remembered when presented through more than one sense e.g. heard & written on the blackboard help better retention than only hearing something
3. **Rehearse and Recite:** Rehearsal & recitation are useful in memorizing thus self evaluation is possible and learning can be modified accordingly.
4. **Space your learning:** Spacing what we learn or distributed learning helps better retention learning as things learnt in small

parts is retained longer.

5. **Follow the principle of association:** Associating what we are learning with what we already know helps in remembering . e.g. A for apple, Z for zebra etc.
6. **Use Correlation:** Topics must not be taught or learnt in water tight compartments thus correlate with experiences & related subjects to make learning interesting.
7. **Grouping & rhythm** e.g. multiplication tables and poems are easy to learn because of grouping & rhythm. Use of Mnemonics also aids learning.
8. **Whole to Part to Whole:** Before intensive study, go through the whole matter, understand it, break it to parts & then study it whole following the whole to part to whole method.
9. **Take breaks:** Periods of change, rest & sleep helps remove fatigue & monotony thus fresh mind stores meaningful experiences for longer time.
10. **Over learn:** Over learning helps retention. Review and revise very often.
11. **Avoid interference of subject similarity:** Interference causes forgetting so similar situations, subjects, etc .must be spaced out. Complete the work, do sufficient drill work & then begin the next learning situation.

12. **Good Environment:** Better learning environment makes learning interesting & vivid by using teaching aids , adopting new methods and techniques.

Check your progress.

1. What is forgetting? What are the causes of forgetting.
2. What are the different ways to minimize forgetting?
3. What are the various ways in which a student can improve the ways in which he learns?

3. IMAGINATION

Imagination is a spontaneous process which occurs when an individual is doing nothing in particular, is not responding to any clearly identifiable stimulus and is relatively passive. It is actually the experience of earlier sensory experiences in the absence of the relevant stimulus. Therefore, imagination is based on one's past experiences. It is through sensation and perception that the knowledge of the world is acquired.

Imagination can also be defined as mental manipulation. These mental manipulations involve recall of past experience in the form of mental images and in arranging them in a pattern to form a new combination. Here the pattern can be made by adding or deleting the images.

A series of images are called Imagery. Imagery could be obtained from any of the five senses. Imagery is the exact replica of the object e.g. when we are asked to have an auditory image of the school bell, one will not imagine the structure of anything apart from the school bell.

<u>Mc Dougall</u>: "Imagination is the thinking of remote objects."

Woodworth: "Imagination is mental manipulation. When the individual recalls facts previously observed in reality and proceeds to arrange these facts into a new pattern, he is said to show imagination."

Thus, imagination represents a very simple and passive type of thinking process. Normally, imagination occurs when one is relatively free and is not particularly directing their attention to any specific problem or issue. It is, in a way, a sort of idle activity.

Types of Imagination

A. Reproductive B) Productive or Constructive Creative Imitative

Pragmatic Aesthetic Fantastic

Imagination mainly occurs in two ways. The imagination that may be the exact copy of the original or may be the original rearranged to create something new altogether thus we get-

A. Reproductive Imagination: The reproductive imagination is a mere repetition of the past experiences. This kind of imagination is considered to be of the lowest form. e.g. When we memories or rote memory it is actual reproduction without any addition or cutout.

B. Productive or Constructive Imagination: When the imagination is altered & restructured & new images are formed is called productive imagination e.g. writing a poem, painting, anything which shows newness or novelty of ideas.

This is sub divided into Creative Imagination, Imitative Imagination

1. Creative Imaginationis when something new is created. There is originality in the creation. It is the very superior kind of imagination. E.g. scientist, artists, novelists, poets, playwrights.

Creative Imagination is again sub divided to

a. Aesthetic imagination- when it is directed to the production and appreciation of beauty. No outside control is accepted. The artist has his own code of laws of working. E.g. an artist or a dancer or a musician.

b. Pragmatic imagination- when the imagination fulfills a practical aspect. E.g. architects designing a building. External control is present.

c. Fantastic type of imagination- many people build castles in the air, in this case, the imagination has no control, there are no conditions applying here.

2. Imitative Imaginationis when creative imagination is used or the original idea is adapted. E.g. when a play is based on the novel or the script becomes film. Thus even readers of science, history, travel books, novel and poetry all exercise imitative imagination.

Check your progress:

1. What is imagination? What are the different types of imagination?

8.4 REASONING

Meaning

Reasoning plays a significant role in one's adjustment to one's environment. It controls not only one's cognitive activities but may also influence the total behavior and personality by the proper or improper development of one's reasoning ability. It is essentially a cognitive ability and is like thinking in many aspects.

Characteristics of reasoning:

1. It has definite goal or purpose.
2. It is implicit act and involves problem solving behavior.
3. It involves the use of one's previous knowledge and experiences.
4. In reasoning, there is mental exploration rather than motor exploration as it involves mental exploration of the reason or cause of an event or happening.
5. It is highly symbolic function. The ability to interpret various symbols, development of concepts and language aids reasoning.

Thus, it can be concluded that reasoning is productive and advanced stage in complex process of thinking. It is more serious and complex mental process.

Garrett: Reasoning is step – wise thinking with a purpose or goal in mind.

Gates:Reasoning is the term applied to highly purposeful, controlled and selective thinking.

Munn:Reasoning is combining past experiences in order to solve a problem which cannot be solved by mere reproduction of earlier solutions.

An analysis of the above definitions reveal that reasoning depicts a higher type of thinking which is a very careful, systematic and organized function. It may follow some logical systematic steps like:

1. Identification of goal or purpose to which the reasoning is to be directed.
2. Mental exploration or search for the various possibilities, cause

– and – effect relationships or solutions for realizing the set goal or purposes based on the previous learning or experiences and present observations or attempts.

3. Selection of the most appropriate possibility or solution by careful mental analysis of all the available alternatives.
4. Testing the validity of the selected possibility or solution, purely through mental exercise and thus finally accepting or rejecting it for the actual solution of the problem.

Thus, reasoning may be termed as highly specialized thinking which helps an individual to explore mentally the cause – and – effect relationship of an event or solution of a problem by adopting some well – organized systematic steps based on previous experiences combined with present observation.

Check your Progress:

1. Define Reasoning. What are its characteristics?

5. LET US SUM UP

- Thinking is a pattern of behavior in which we make use of internal representations (symbols, signs etc.) of things and events for the solution of some specific, purposeful problem.
- We think with the help of Percepts, Images / Object, Concepts, Symbols / Signs, and Language.
- **Thinking can be** Convergent (one best answer from many sources), Divergent (different ideas from a source), Critical (assessing the worth and validity of something), Reflective (insightful cognitive thinking), or Lateral (thinking out of the box).

- Memory is the ability to retain & reproduce impressions once perceived
- Types of Memory are Immediate (few seconds), Short term (upto thirty seconds if not chunked or coded) and Permanent (for a fairly long time).
- Retention can be measured through the Recall method, the Recognition method and the Relearning method.
- Registration or learning is done through rote memorization, spacing out the learning material, using whole or part learning, recitation and using mnemonics.
- Forgetting is the inability to find the correct information (from our memory) at the given situation. It can be temporary or permanent.
- Imagination is a passive, idle time activity based on past experiences. Imagination can be Reproductive or Productive. Productive Imagination can be further be Creative (Pragmatic/ Aesthetic/ Fantastic) or Imitative.
-

Reasoning is step – wise thinking with a purpose or goal in mind.

6. GLOSSARY

Thinking: the mental exploration for finding out the solution of a problem.

Memory: the retention or storage of information in any form.

Forgetting: the inability to find the correct information (from our memory) at the given situation.

Imagination: an idle, passive activity based on previous experience in which one thinks of remote objects.

Reasoning: a highly purposeful, controlled, selective and step by step thinking

????

CHAPTER-9

PERSONALITY

Unit Structure

0. Objectives
1. Introduction
2. Personality

1. Definitions of Personality
2. Characteristics of Personality
3. Traditional theories of personality type theory
4. Trait theory

3. Self-Concept
4. Mental Health

1. Characteristics of mental health
2. Importance of Mental health

5. Maladjustment

1. Causes of Maladjustment
2. Preventive measures of maladjustment

0. OBJECTIVES

After going through this unit, you will able to

- understand the meaning and nature of personality
- Distinguish between type & theories of personality.
- Understand the concept of 'self-concept'
- Understand the meaning of mental health
- Describe characteristics of mental health.
- Understand importance of mental health
- Understand concept of maladjustment
- List out causes of maladjustment
- List out preventive measures of maladjustment

1. INTRODUCTION:

In child centered education child has been given utmost important. Child's personality plays major role in teaching learning

process. Personality is often misused in describing outer appearance of the person. Personality is more than that. It covers inner as well as outer look. Attitude aptitude reflects in the type of personality. Importance of mental health, role of school and teachers in improving personality / adjustment is discussed in this block.

2. PERSONALITY

Personality is the whole individual considered as a whole. It may be defined as "the most characteristic integration of an individual structure, modes of interest, attitudes, behavior and capacities.

MUIRHEAD

Personality is a term that has been used very widely but each time to mean some different aspects of a person. Every society and in it every school, takes a profound interest in the development of the personality of children. Etymologically, the word 'personality' has been derived from the Latin word 'Persona'. At first this word was used for the mask worn by the actors to change their appearance but later on, it began to be used for the actors themselves. Since then, the term 'personality' has been used to depict outward appearance or external behavior etc.

1. : Definitions of the personality:

- N.L.Munn – 'Personality may be defined as the most characteristic – integration of an individual's structure, modes of behavior, interest, attitudes, capacities, abilities and aptitudes'.
- C.V.Good – 'The total psychological and social reaction of an individual, the synthesis of his subjective, emotional and mental life.
- Valentine – 'Personality is the sum total of innate and acquired dispositions'.

2. : Characteristics of personality:

Personality has got certain important characteristics, they are:

1. Personality is always dynamic
2. Personality determines our thinking, reasoning and actions.
3. personality is both physical and psychological (outer and inner).
4. Personality develops through social interaction.
5. Every personality has some uniqueness.
6. Personality has organized and integrated system.
7. Personality refers to the process of adjustment to our environment.

In short:

P- Perception capacity E- Emotional maturity

R- Responsiveness to situations S- Self-expression or sociability O- Organized

N- Not permanent (Flexible) A- Appearance

L- Leadership feeling I- Integrated

T- Tendencies, impulses, dispositions, innate & acquired Y- young, vital and unique

No two individuals are alike and that is what makes life interesting and exciting. The emphasis is on growth and development that on genetic endowment.

3. : Traditional Theories of Personality

Type Theory

Galen's Classification

Humours or Fluids

Temperament

Personality

Blood

Sanguine

Active, Hopeful

Yellow Bile

Choleric

Irritable, Easily provoked

Phlegm

Phlegmatic (Lethargic)

Dull, sluggish

Black Bile

Malancholic

Depressed and

Ernest Kretshmer, a German Psychiatrist classified human beings on the basis of physical constitution.

Type

Bodily Features

Personality

Asthenic

Slender, Weak

Moody & withdrawn

Pyknic

Shor, Round and Fat

Jovial & Outgoing

Atheletic

Strong, Sturdy and Well proportioned

Well adjusted

Dr.William Scheldon's Classification

Body Type

Temperamental Types

Endomorphy (Round, Fat & Soft)

Viscerotonia

(Love of physical comfort, Sociable affectionate)

Mesomorphy

(Heavy muscular build)

Somatotonia

(Energetic, Assertive)

Ambitious

&

Ectomorphy

(Long, Slender & Poor muscular development)

Cerebrotonia

(Restrained, withdrawn)

thoughtful

and

Spranger's Classification

Types

Interests

The Theoretical

Intellectual, pursuit, Discovery of Truth

The Economic

Pragmatic, Marketing transactions

The Aesthetic

Lover of Beauty and Art

The Social

Human relationship and altruism

The Political

Power and Influence

The religious

Ultimate meaning as Unity in life in terms of higher power

4. : Later Theories of Personality Trait Theory

G.W.Allport defines personality trait as "A trait is a neuropsychic structure having the capacity to render many stimuli functionally equivalent and to initiate and guide equivalent forms of adaptive and expressive behavior" (1961)

R.B.Cattell attempted a classification beginning with 171 traits and subsequently narrowing with 171 traits and subsequently narrowing them down to 35 and finally to only 12

These are as follows:

1. Cyclothymia – Such a person is Frank emotional and given to a very frank expression of his views.
2. General mental capacity – An average level of intelligence.

3. Dominance – self-confident, assertive and quarrelsome
4. Sergency – Humour, intelligence
5. Positive character – A person of this native gives special attention to the view of others.
6. Emotionally stable – they don't suffer from instability
7. Adventurous cyclothymia – Adventurous, inclined to mix easily with others.
8. Mature – Independent, mature and complete in themselves.
9. Socialised cultured – Give special attention to thoughts about the age in which they live.
10. Trustful – Trustful and grateful to others
11. Unconventional – Revolt against the times in which they live.
12. Sophisticated – Rational, reasonable, peaceable and inclined towards solitude.

Check you progress

1. What is characteristics o personality?
2. Distinguish between type and trait theories of personality.

3. SELF CONCEPT:

Definition – Psychologically, the whole set of attitudes opinions and cognitions that a person has of him.

Self-concept is a multidimensional construct that refers to an individual's perception of 'self' in relation to any number of characteristics.

Such as academics (and non-academics), gender roles and sexuality, racial identity and many others. The idea of self-concept is utilized in many disciplines including psychology, philosophy, sociology, nursing, biology and anthropology, there is no consensus as to how to define "Self-concept using terms of specificity.

At present the development of self-concept among the students is worrying. Most students have low self-concept and they are so passive achievements in school.

According to Gadeyne, E, Ghesquiere, P, & Onghene P. (2004) to develop the students positive self-concept, parents need to provide a harmonious household climate, full of happiness and have adequate necessities. While teachers in schools also need to provide a conducive learning environment and be sensitive to the psychological needs of the students.

According to Azizi etal (2005). Any man has a picture or perception of himself. This includes looks and appearance, physical health, ability, weakness and his behavior. Thus self-concept is how one evaluates or judges himself that is either in a positive or negative way. Self-concept can be classified into two major types that are positive self-concept and negative self-concept. The positive self-concept is about a circumstance or situation in which an individual is confident and sure of him, have good interests, be objective and not too sensitive. A negative self-concept is when an individual has too subjective nature.

Check your progress

1. How will you describe self-concept?

4. MENTAL HEALTH

One of the most important aims of education is to help the individual in making adjustment with the changing environment. It is the mental health which helps the person to adjust in the environment.

Mental health stands for the health of the mind an Carter V. Good in the dictionary of Education (1959 P. 263) has termed it as. "The wholesomeness of the mind."

It is a state or condition on which an individual feels a sense of wellbeing. This condition also provides an individual the capacity to be resilient to the stresses her / meets and to respond to these challenges without having to compromise his well-being. This also makes him productive and fruitful for himself and his community.

WHO defines mental health as – A state of complete physical, mental and social well-being and not merely the absence of disease or infirmity (2001).

Definition – A state of emotional and psychological wellbeing in which an individual is able to use his or her cognitive and emotional capabilities function in society, and meet the ordinary demands of everyday life.

1. : Characteristics of mental health:

1. Nothing called perfect mental health – No person is with perfect mental health rather it is optimum mental health.
2. Mental health is a dynamic concept: Mental health denotes a state of balance or equilibrium of our mind, this balance is not static, it is quite dynamic.
3. Mental health can't be achieved without physical health-for achieving an optimal level of mental health one has to first acquire adequate physical health.
4. Mental health and efficiency are not the same thing – One may be quite efficient and successful at his work or profession but he could be most unhappy, full of anxiety etc.
5. Mental health and social ability are not the same thing- A mentally healthy person is sociable it is not necessary for a sociable or socially adaptable person to be healthy minded.

6. Mental health differs from ethical standards – Morality does not guarantee mental health.

Check you progress:

1. what are the characteristics of mental health

2. : <u>Importance of Mental Health</u>-

Mental health has much wider scope than physical health as it aims for the development of wholesome balanced and integrated personality.

Mental health is very important because of following things:

1. <u>Helps in the development of desirable personality</u> – Mental health helps in the development of a wholesome, well-balanced and integrated personality.
2. <u>Helps in proper emotional development</u> – The individual who enjoy good mental health are supposed to demonstrate proper emotional maturity in their behaviors. On the other side, those who are tense, disintegrated and mentally unhealthy demonstrate sudden emotional outburst.
3. <u>Helps in proper social development</u>- Ones mental health helps one in becoming sociable and establishing proper social relationships in the society.
4. <u>Helps in proper moral development</u> – The individuals who enjoy sound mental health are usually found to behave as a man of integrity and character by following the ethical standards of the society.
5. <u>Helps in proper aesthetic development</u> – Proper mental health helps the individual in the development of appropriate aesthetic sense, artistic taste and refined temperament.
6. <u>Helps in seeking proper adjustment</u> – A mentally healthy individual is an adjusted person. He is able to adjust his needs as per the demands of the situation and well being of the society.
7. <u>Helps in seeking goals of life</u> – Optimum mental health always helps the individuals to divert his energies in full capacity for the realization of the goals.
8. <u>Helps in progress of the society</u> – Mental health helps the individual to develop as well balanced useful citizens who are conscious not only of their rights but also of their responsibilities.
9. <u>Helps in prevention of mental illness</u> – A sound mental health and balanced personality has enough resistance to fight against

the odds of life and bear the accidental stresses and strains of life in comparison to those with impaired mental health.

Check you progress

1. Elucidate importance of mental health.

5. MALADJUSTMENT:

Adjustment is the process by which a living organism maintains a balance between its needs and the circumstances that influence the satisfaction of these needs. An individual's adjustment is adequate, wholesome or healthy to the extent that he has established harmonious relationship between himself and the conditions, situations and persons who comprise his physical and social environment.

Maladjustment refers to disharmony between the person and his environment. Contrary to adjustment, maladjustment represents a condition or state in which one feels that one's needs are not fulfilled and he has been a failure in establishing harmony with his self and the environment.

1. : Causes of maladjustments:

The causes of one's maladjustment to his self and the environment may be both of personal as well as environmental

Following are the causes of maladjustment:

1. **Unhealthy home environment** – It is because of separated family, divorced family, step mother or step father, drunkard or addicted parents, single parenting and low moral and social standard of family.

2. **Heredity causes** – One may feel inferior because of inherit defective mental set up, physiological structure, color of the skin (dark) which leads to maladjustment.

3. **Poverty** – when poor children meet rich children in the school, they sometimes develop jealousy, worry and inferiority complex which lead to emotional disturbance.

4. **Environment causes** – The forces of environment begin to play their role right from the conception of the child in the womb of the mother in the form of defective nourishment available to him. Uncongenial physical environment, adverse physical environment. Leads to maladjustment.

5. **Faulty method of teaching** – Faulty method of teaching do not motivate students. Lesson become dull and drudgery. Student

begin to hate every process of education. It creates emotional tension which lead to mental illness.

6. **Strict Discipline** – Some traditional schools impose strict discipline, such schools are just like jails and the teachers jailors. Those students are always suffering form fear and worry.

7. **Lack of equipments (facility)**- In some schools, there is lack of furniture and proper equipments. Overcrowded classes and poor facilities leads to frustration and mental tension.

8. **Lack of guidance and counseling** – Mastery over content and subject matter only without caring for the interest of students. No guidance is provided for various areas at different levels. Students became confused, frustrated and become maladjusted.

9. **Lack of recreational facilities** – children who do not get facilities after class room in the forms of play, library, debates, discussion, puzzles etc. may hinder adjustment.

10. **Massmedia** – children are exposed to mass media, explosion of knowledge, adult issues now days. It the child witness films which depict low sexuality and violence. It may lead to maladjustment.

11. **Social laws and bindings** – The social laws and legal binding are the most common source of frustrations in one's life. Similarly restrictions imposed by parents, teachers, ethical and other groups are a common sources of maladjustment.

12. **Bad company / neighbourhood** – Neighbourhood is an important conditioner of child's behavior. Many of our youngsters develop delinquencies because such patterns of behavior are available in their neighbourhood patterns like lying, stealing, obscene talk, promjscuous sex interest.

2. : Preventice measures of Maladjustment

Following are the measures which prevent maladjustment;

1. **Proper encouragement** – Parents and teachers should speak daily with the child about his daily activities. So the child can begin to learn the principles of socialization.
2. **Proper appreciation** – Parents and teachers should directly praise the child for good things he has done.

3. **Delegating responsibility** – Parents and teachers should assign some responsibility to the child. This responsibility should evolve tasks which child perceives as real and important.

4. **Provision of entertainment** – Provide entertainment facilities like parks, sports clubs, amusement places, theaters, museum to children. We should encourage the child to engage in play with his peers.

5. **Testing** – Refer the child for special education testing in some instances maladjusted children and eligible for special education services.

6. **Pattern of relaxation** – The teacher should set a pattern of calmness, yoga, meditation, stress management courses plays very important roles in preventing maladjustment.

7. **Informing progress** – Teacher should inform the child of the progress he is making.

8. **Timely help** – Teacher should help the child when he needs it and not only when he asks for it. If the teacher is wise enough to know when the child requires help, he may be able to help him avoid many traumatic failure experiences.

9. **Moral Education** – School should provide value education through various methods. Self-confidence, co-operation, caring and sharing are the values can be inculcated through co- curricular programmes.

10. **Guidance and counseling** – If teacher works as guide and counselor for parents and children, many of the negative situations can be turned into positive one which is benefited to students.

Check your progress:

1. Describe concept of maladjustment
2. List out causes of maladjustment
3. list out preventive measures of maladjustment.

????

CHAPTER-10

INTELLIGENCE

Unit Structure

0. Objectives
1. Introduction
2. Concept of Intelligence
3. Nature of Intelligence
4. Functions of Intelligence
5. Measurements of intelligence
6. Uses of Intelligence tests
7. Let us sum-up

0. OBJECTIVE

After completing this unit you should be able to:

- Define the concept of intelligence.
- Describe the functions of intelligence.
- State the uses of intelligence tests.
- Test the intelligence by using intelligence tests.

1. INTRODUCTION

You know that every individual is a unique being. Along with the features and characteristics shared with over people, i.e. the universal ones, each individual had many particular characteristics. The individual is born as a man, but only gradually with the help of adults and through his own activity, becomes an individual. As for the adult's influence, the decisive role in this process is played by education which is purposeful, planned, professional and institutionalized. However, the development of the individual is influenced both by internal and external influences. In the process of education and development of personality, the pupil is not only the object of education but also the subject of his own development. These subjective tendencies are intelligence, attitude, aptitude, creativity and interest which are particularly the concern of psychology.

This unit deals with the inner ability of the individual like intelligence which makes one different from other. As we have discussed no two organisms are exactly alike. From birth onward, differences become increasingly apparent, especially in human beings,

partly as expressions of here dietary factor and partly through the impact of the environment. Such differences have been recognized since ancient times and they occur in all human abilities including intellectual functions.

You must have observed that two individuals who study the same amount of time for an examination achieve different scores. You also know that some succeed in medical school while others have difficulty even finishing high school. Then question may arise in your mind why this thing happens? Your response to these questions might be that high intelligence leads to success.

Intelligence is one of the most widely used yet most widely debated concepts in scientific and everyday life. Intelligence means different things to different people. Rob showed many intelligent behaviors when working through computer programmes or recalling sports statistics, but he was unable to express his ideas and knowledge of English literature clearly on examination. Many psychologists believe that intelligence does not refer to one special ability but to a group of abilities. All the definitions offered by psychologists share certain concepts. Let us discuss about the concept of intelligence in detail.

2. CONCEPT ON INTELLIGENCE

The word intelligence forms part of own ordinary stock of words which we use everyday. In the field of psychology too, the word intelligence finds a fairly comprehensive use. In fact, there are as many definitions of intelligences as there are writers on the subject. On account of the different ways in which intelligence is interpreted, it has become less acceptable and more exposed to criticism by psychologists. Nevertheless, it is traditionally acknowledged by the parents and teachers that intelligence is the most important single variable which affects success in school and in life. In general terms, intelligence means the manner with which an individual deals with facts and situations. First, intelligence is defined interns of observable objective behavior. Second, most definitions refer both to an individual's capacity to learn and to knowledge that has already been acquired. Many definitions also suggest that the ability to adapt to the environment is a sign of intelligence.

A variety of definitions on intelligence have been suggested by the psychologists who can be classified into at least four distinct groups as follows.

INTELLIGENCE

Ability to Adjust

According to this group, intelligence is general mental adaptability to new problems and new situations of life. Some definitions come under this group are as follows.

Binet (1905): "Intelligence is the ability of an individual to direct his behavior towards a goal".

William James (1907): "It is the ability to adjust oneself successfully to a relatively new situation'.

J. Piagel (1926): "Intelligence is an adaptations to physical and social environment".

F. N. Freeman (1937); "Intelligence is represented in behavior by the capacity of the individual to adjust himself to new situations to solve new problems to learn."

Ability to Learn

This group of definitions of Intelligence stresses the ability to learn. The more intelligent the person, the more readily and extensively he is able to learn and enlarge his field of activity and experience is the key words of these definitions.

Buckingham (1921) "Intelligence is the learning ability."

Superman (1927) "Intelligence may be though of interns of two abilities i.e. "g" or general and 's' or specific."

Thurstone (1946) "Defines intelligence interns of five primary abilities i.e. 'S' or space factor, 'N' or number factor 'V' or Verbal Comprehension factor, 'W' or word fluency factor and 'M' or memory factor."

Ability to do abstract reasoning

This group of definitions maintains that intelligence is the ability to carry on abstruct thinking. This implies the effective use of ideas and efficiency in dealing with symbols, specially numerical and verbal symbols.

L. M. Termon (1921): "An individual is intelligent in proportion as he is able to carry on abstract thinking."

P. E. Vernon (1927): "Intelligence is an allround thinking capacity or mental deficiency."

E. L. Thornlike (1931): "we may define intelligence in general as the power of good responses from the point of view of truth or fact."

Henry Garrel (1946): "Intelligence is the abilities demanded in the solution of problems which require the comprehension and use of symbols i.e. words, numbers diagrams, equations, formula."

Operational definition

These categories of definitions are not and perhaps can not be mutually exclusive.

They intersect and overlap at many points.

P. E. Vernon (1927) "Intelligence is what intelligence test measures."

G. D. Stoddard (1943) "Intelligence is the ability to undertake activities."

Boring (1948) "Intelligence is what intelligence tests".

D. W. Wechster (1950) "Intelligence is the aggregate or the global capacity of the individual to act purposefully, to think rationally and to deal effectively with the environment."

Evaluating on the basis of the above definition, we can call a person intelligent in proportion to his being able to use his mental energy in handing his actual life problems and leading a happy and well contented life.

Check Your Progress:

Note: Write down answer in the space given below:

I. Write two definitions to prove that intelligence is an ability to learn.
II. Write the definition of intelligence according to Binet.
III. In defining intelligence Thurstone and Spearnan both used the letter 'S'. What is the meaning of 'S' according to them?

3. NATURE OF INTELLIGENCE

I am sure that you got idea about what intelligence is. Now we will discuss the nature of intelligence. You may have the experience of discussing about the nature of your friends, parents, teachers etc., but today you will get the joy of discussing the nature of intelligence which changes the nature of persons.

The nature of intelligence was first though of by a brilliant English Scientist Sir Francis Galton. His general conclusion that intelligence is a hereditary trait is reflected by the title of his book "Hereditary Genius."

As you see that the definition of intelligence is defined differently, so the nature of intelligent is also described by different persons in different ways. For example the school teacher may describe a student as bright, if the learns his lesson easily. The manager of a Super Bazar may regard a Salesman as intelligent and smart if he can satisfy customers and dispose them of quickly. The workshops manager may regard an apprentice as intelligence if the he is skillful in using his hands and his tools. In the above cases, the word 'intelligent' has been used in the sense of "efficient behavior."

The nature of intelligence also differs according to the nature of work if can do. For example handing ideas and symbols such as words, formulas, numbers and diagrams abstract intelligence is required. A person with abstract intelligence is able to discover relations among symbols and to solve problems. Professionals like doctors, lawyers, literary men as well as business men and statesmen are supposed to possess a high degree of abstract intelligent.

In the same way the ability to deal with machines, equipment and mechanical appliances requires mechanical intelligence. The mechanics, the engineer and the trained industrial worker are supposed to be mechanically intelligence.

Efficiency in getting on well in personal and social affairs requires social intelligence. Salesmen, Diplomats and Ministers are supposed to be socially intelligent. The socially intelligent person makes friends easily and is fateful in dealing with human beings. In selecting people for different occupations it is useful to know the types of intelligence an applicant possesses.

There are, however, gross variations in the three different types of intelligence not only from person to person but also within the same person. A boy may not be able to learn mathematics but may be ingenious in using mechanical tools. A girl may find chemistry and physics uninteresting but may have the talent to master a foreign language. We do not usually find a student who is very good in one subject and poor in all other subjects. It is rare to find a person who can do only one task very well. On the other hand, it may be found that even average people perform to be positively related, we have discussed on the concept & nature of intelligence. On that basis we can generalize the important nature & characteristics of intelligence as follows.

Intelligence is inherited

The amount of intelligence that a person possesses in inherited and fixed. The amount though fixed does not reveal itself at the start of life with the growth of the child, the amount inherited by a child also grows. The general belief is that the growth of intelligence stops and it reaches it's limit at the age of sixteen. But you know and it is also true that a man of forty knows more than he was a boy of sixteen. But this does not mean that the amount of intelligence possessed by him has increased. This may be due to his experience. As regards his intelligence, his positions remains the same.

Intelligence is influenced by environment factors

Love, affection, concern & generosity judiciously bestowed on growing children, have very desirable effects. Poor environment retard development of intelligence.

Intelligence helps in adjustment & inventions

An intelligent person has the ability to adjust himself to the changing circumstances with ease, efficiency and speed. He has the capacity to assimilate ideas very quickly and clearly. He can cope? With new situations very successfully. All the inventions of the word can be attributed to persons of very high intelligence.

Intelligence has no sex differences

Various studies have been conducted by psychologists & researcher a to find out whether women are more intelligent that men and vice versa. The result of these researches hangs in one way or the other. In some of the cases no significant difference has been found. Research studies also so that the average scores of the sense are strongly similar.

Therefore it is proper to think that difference in sex does not contribute towards difference in intelligence.

Intelligence has no racial or cultural differences

Now, students we will see whether a particular race, caste or cultural group is superior to other in intelligence. This hypothesis are also examined by so many research workers, the results of earlier studies proved that intelligence is not the birth right of particular race of group. The bright and the 'dull' can be found in any race, caste or cultural group. In this regard Franze Boas states. "If we were to select the most intelligent, imaginative, energetic and emotionally stable third of mankind, all races would be represented. "you can also take any study & prove if."

Intelligence can be recognized in three broad areas

Students, you know that all the individuals are not same in their physical appearance. Here you will also able to know that all people are not having same type and same amount of intelligence in solving all problems. According to Thurstone intelligent behavior can be recognized in three broad areas.

Abstract Intelligence Abstract intelligence is the ability

to understand and manage ideas and symbols. Such as words, numbers etc. In the case of students this is very close to scholastic aptitude.

Mechanical Intelligence Mechanical intelligence is the

ability to clean, understand and manage things and mechanisms, such as a knife, a gun, a moving machine and automobile etc.

Social Intelligence social intelligence is the ability to understand and mange men and women, boys and girls, to act wisely in human relations.

Functions of Intelligence:

Intelligence directs one's behavior towards a goal. It helps one to adjust to a new situations.

It helps an individual to adopt to physical and social environment.

It helps to learn new things and to solve new problems.

It directs the individual to think rationally and act purposefully.

Check Your Progress II

Note: Fill in the blanks.

I. The nature of intelligence was first though by a brilliant

.... Scientist Sir ....

II. Intelligent is a hereditary trait is reflected by the title of the book ....

III. The German psychologist .... introduced the concept of I. Q,

10.5 MEASUREMENT OF INTELLIGENCE

You know that to measure something we need a unit a measure. For example to measure the length we use a scale, weighing machine for measuring weight etc. To know how much of anything exists, we have to measure it. So in your mind question may arise to know how much intelligence you have? Do you know how to measure it? Can you measure it through kilogram, kilometer, litre, scale or other measure like this? No, to measure the amount of intelligence, there is no such one specific measuring scale. Because intelligence is not an object, it is not observable, but it is a relative mental ability. Though it can not be measured directly though any single unit of measure, still if can be measured. Let us discuss how intelligence can also be measured. Al of you may be very curious to know if.

It is important to note that intelligence is inferred from a variety of elements i.e. behavior and speed of doing things correctly etc. In ancient India intelligence was measured through conversation, physical features, gestures, gait, speech, changes in the eye and facial expression. But today, many intelligence tests are widely which primarily measures abstract intelligence as exemplified by competence in dealing with symbols in a meaningful way. A number of tests measuring social intelligence as well as mechanical intelligence have also been developed. An intelligence test is an objective and a standard measure.

General (or abstract) Intelligence test

The general intelligence test was first designed by psychologists for use in schools. These were intended to serve primarily as tools in determining a child's ability to carry on schools work, to use symbols and numbers quickly and accurately and to read with comprehension. It is for this reason that tests designed to measure abstract abilities came to be known as general intelligence tests.

Another purpose of designing such tests was to measure the abilities that distinguishes the bright child from the dull. Since this distinction is significant for schools and vocational success and also for social adjustment, the intelligence test is an important tool in psychology.

Types of Intelligence Test

The general intelligence tests have been classified into three groups. Individual, group and performance tests.

Performance

Group

Individual

Types of Intelligence Test

Non - Verbal

Verbal

Individual Test:

The individual intelligence test is administered to only one individual at a time. A trained psychologist is expected to administer the test for a definite period of time and interpret the result. These tests cover age group from 2 years to 18 years. These are (iO The Binet simon tests, (ii) Revised tests by Terman, (iii) Mental scholastic tests of Burt and (d) Weschler test.

Group Test:

The group intelligence tests are meant for assessing the intelligence of a large number of individuals in one sitting. There are two kinds of group intelligence tests verbal and nonverabal.

Verbal:

The verbal group test requires an individuals to read out certain problems and write out solutions of these problems.

Non-Verbal:

The non-verbal group tests presents similar problems as the verbal test but in a different way. The problems are presented in the form of pictures, diagrams, puzzles and mazes. If does not require the individual to read or write, but only to be able to make a mark with a pencil.

Performance Test

Performance tests are designed to test problem solving ability using certain objects such as pictures and blocks, instead of words. These tests are especially useful with young children, illiterates, persons with speech defects and persons who do not have proficiency in language. Some of the famous tests are (i) Koh's Block design test (ii) The cube construction tests and (iii) The Pass Along tests.

Group tests had their birth in America when the intelligence of the recruits who joined the army in the first world war was to be calculated. These are (i) The Army Alpha and Beta test (ii) Terman's group tests, (iii) Out self-administrative tests.

Intelligence tests consists of different types of questions to test the intelligence of individual. These questions are based on the following factors.

Vocabulary

The extent of an individual's vocabulary is one of the most reliable indices of his intelligence. It can be tested through arranging words in difficult order or giving synonym or antonym of a word.

Verbal analogies:

In this section question are asked like Branch is to a tree as brook is to river.

Sentence completion :

India has..................... states is one of the example of this type

of questions.

Arithmetic reasoning:

Simple arithmetical sum increasing in difficulty is included in the test.

Number series:

A series of number is given and asked what will be the next?

For example 11, 13, 15, 17, 19, 21................. ?

Comprehension:

It consists of questions designed to measure general understanding. It includes questions such as why are coins made of metal?

Digit Span:

For testing on memory, digits are spoken and the subject is asked to respect them in the same or reverse order. For example if the examiner says 8, 4, 3 the subject is to say 3, 4, 8.

Similarities:

The subject is asked to describe the way in which certain objects are similar. In way cotton and silk are a like?

General Information:

If consists of questions from everyday life. Kinds of questions asked. How many inches are there in a foot?

Picture arrangement:

Each item consists of a collection of cartoon like drawings which make a story when arranged in proper order.

Picture completion:

This test consists of a series of pictures which are presented to the subject one at a time. An important part is missing from each picture and must be identified by the subject.

Block design:

The subject must arrange a collection of colored cubes in such a way that they reproduce certain printed design.

Object assembly test.

Three jigsaw type puzzles are presented to the subject one at a time and in order of increasing difficulty.

Digit symbol test:

The subject is required to match each one of series of printed digits with an appropriate symbol, using a prescribed code.

These are different verbal and non-verbal factors on which questions are framed to test the intelligence of the individual. But this process of determining the intelligence is a complicated process. It involves a comparison and establishment of a relationship between chronological age (C. A.) and mental age (M. A.). This relationship is expressed by the term I. Q. (Intelligent Quotient) Now we will discuss the concept of age, chronological age & intelligent quotient.

Mental Age:

In categorizing children of different abilities Binet developed a scale of units he called mental age. A Child's intelligence was determined by the mental age level which he could attain on the test.

A ten years old child who was able to all the tests meant for ten years old children was said to be normal or average. If he could do the test meant for a higher age level his mental age was said to be more than his chronological age and he was described as a bright child. If he was unable to do the tests meant for his own age level, the child's "mental age" was said to be lower than his chronological age and he was described as slow or retarded. Mental age is a simple and useful concept. You can easily interpret it, when deal with children differing in metal ability.

Chronological Age: (C. A.)

Chronological age is nothing but the actual calendar age of the child. The real age of the child in mental into consideration for test is called chronological age.

Intelligent quotient:

The intelligent quotient represents the degree of brightness possessed by an individual. It expresses intelligent as the ratio of the metal age of the chronological age. When the mental age is divided by the chronological age and the quotient is multiplied by 100 the result is I. Q. So the formula of finding out I. Q is.

I. Q. = M. A. ? 100

C. A.

The fraction is multiplied by 100 in order to remove the decimal point and to give the I. Q. a value of 100 when mental age is equal with chronological age. This if the M. A. is above the C. A.

I. Q. will be above 100. If the M. A. is less than the C. A. the resulting I. Q. will be less than 100. thus the scale has the same meaning from one age to another. I. Q, may also be regarded as an index of brightness. The following table shows the relationship between I.Q. and the degree of brightness given by Dr. Merrily based on the studies by Terman Merely Revision.

I. Q. Range	Classification	Percentage of populations
140 and above	Very superior	1.5
129 -139	Superior	11
110 – 119	High - Average	18
90 – 109	Average	47
80 – 89	Low Average	14
70 – 79		

Borderline defective

6

Below 70

Mentally defective

2.5

The lowest classification mentally defective sometimes subdivided into three classes as:

Moron I.Q. – 50 – 70

Imbecility I. Q. – 20 – 50 Idiot I. Q. – Below 20

Thus you can use the intelligence tests already developed or you can also prepare an intelligence tests of measure the intelligence of an individual.

Check Your Progress – 3

1. What type of Intelligence test can be used to test the intelligent of illiterate and language handicap children? Give two examples.
2. Write the formula of find gone I. Q,
3. Why 100 is multiplied in the formula of I. Q.?

You know how to test the intelligence of others, but what you will do after knowing the intelligence level others? If there is no use of knowing the intelligence of others, there is no need of measuring if. Therefore, now we will see in what way intelligence tests help us and in which areas we can use this knowledge.

Intelligence tests have been put to many uses in now a days. It has been observed that intelligence has much to do with success airfare in making adjustment to life situations and infect, in every department of human activity. Some of the important areas in which intelligence tests may be used are:

Educational uses:

In educational situations intelligence tests helps in:

Selection of Courses:

Selection of courses for pupils can be made on the basis of intelligence tests. Some subjects required higher order of intelligence and other require low order of intelligence. A nationwide study conducted in the United states gave the following median I.

Q. of the high school boys in different courses.

Courses	Median I. Q.
Technical	114
Scientific	108
Academic	106
Commercial	104
Trade	102

Selection of pupils to Schools:

In good school there is always a rush of admission. All the applicants though eligible for admission can not be admitted. In this case, intelligence tests help a lot to meet out this difficulty.

Classification of pupils:

Children can be classification into various categories on the basis of intelligence tests. We have children who are of superior intelligence, average, intelligence, dull and feeble minded. Children having the same I. Q. may be grouped together and constitute a class. This helps in avoiding educational wastage and developing progress among children according to their ability.

Detections of various types of pupils:

In order to classify the pupil into homogeneous group, we have to detect them. This can be done with the help of intelligence tests.

Award of Scholarships:

On the basis of intelligence and achievement tests scholarship may be awarded to suitable candidates.

Promotion of pupils:

Intelligence tests are also used to promote pupils. In case of gifted child, we give double promotion.

Prediction of success :

Student's success can be predicted on the basis of intelligence tests.

Assessment of Teacher's work:

The achievement of students when compared to their intelligence indicates the teacher's work.

Evaluation of Methods and Instructional Material:

Intelligence tests also help in evaluating the importance of different methods & reading materials relating to different subject & text books.

Educational Guidance:

Educational guidance like selection of courses, streams etc, can be given to students on the basis of the results of intelligence tests.

Vocational uses:

Intelligence tests may be of great use in Vocational guidance. Vocational guidance can be given on the basis of the result of intelligence tests.

Uses in Army and Civil Services:

Intelligence tests are extensively used in the Army since the First World War. Army Alpha and Army Beta tests have used on lakhs of persons.

Uses in Industry:

Intelligence tests very useful in Industry in the selection of individuals for particular positions in the industry, in locating workers who require training and to study working conditions. They are also used together with other methods of selection like interview and application forms containing data of previous experience and qualifications.

Uses in Research:

Intelligence tests are very useful for research in selecting the area of research etc.

Uses in the study of National and racial differences:

Intelligence tests have their utility in making survey of recial groups. It helps to know the intelligence level of various races and nationalities. Intelligence test scores show that I. Q. scores of Germans, Japanese and Americans are more than those of African and Mexicans.

There are some of the important tasks of Intelligence tests. But while using the tests. Great care and many precautions are to be observed. Tests should be administered by well-trained persons. Results should be interpreted with care. Test scores should not be taken to be absolutely reliable as tests are by no means prefect.

They should have their limits of usefulness. We require to know much more about the individual than revealed by intelligence tests to make any decision about him.

Check Your Progress - 4

1. Write any three uses of intelligence tests relating to education.
2. Write other two areas besides education, where intelligence tests are also used.

10.7 LET US SUM UP

You would recall that we have touched upon the following learning items in this unit. Intelligence is a mental trait which expresses it self in various forms. It is an inborn natural power. It helps a man in learning things and to solve complicated and comprehend problems and situations. Intelligence can be measured by different types of intelligence tests like individual, group, verbal, nonverbal and performance tests of intelligence.

Intelligence is measured through a complicated process which involves a compression and establishment of a relationship between chronological age and mental age. It is expresses by the term I. Q. Intelligence quotients.

Intelligence tests are used in solving educational problems with the help of intelligence tests, occupational, social and personal guidance can be easily furnished. These tests are, however, required to be use with great care and caution and only by expert in the field.

Unit end Exercises: 1.

i. "Intelligence is the learning ability" – Buckingham "Intelligence may be thought to interns of two abilities i.e. 'g' or general and 's' or specific".

ii. "Intelligence is the ability of an individual to direct his behavior towards a goal".
iii. 'S' – Special ability – Spearman 'S' – Space factor – Thurs stone

2.

i. English, Francis Gallon
ii. Hereditary Genius
iii. Stern

3. Nonverbal intelligence Test, Picture Completion Test and

i. Picture drawing test

ii.

I.Q. = M.A. ×100 C.A

iii. In order to remove the decimal point.

4.00

i. Admission, Promotion & Classification
ii. Vocation, Research

Exercises:

1. Explain the meaning and nature of intelligence.
2. Explain the different types of intelligence tests with examples.
3. Write Short note on the following questions (In 150 words)

a. Uses of intelligence tests.
b. Intelligent quotient.
c. Functions of intelligence.
d. Performance test of intelligence.

Reference books

Dr. S. S. Mathur (1996) Educational Psychology Nerman L. Munn (1967) Introduction to Psychology

G. D. Boaz (1959) General Psychology

????

CHAPTER-11

CREATIVITY

Unit Structure

0. Objectives
1. Introduction
2. Concept of Creativity

1. Definition of Creativity

3. Nature and Characteristics of Creativity
4. Characteristics of Creative Personality
5. Process of Creativity
6. Measurement of Creativity
7. Uses of Creativity test
8. Let us Sum up

0. OBJECTIVE

After reading this unit you will be able to.

- Define Creativity
- Explain the Characteristics of Creativity
- State the Characteristics of a Creative person
- Tell the uses of Creativity tests
- Test of Creativity by using creativity tests.
- Suggests the various ways and means for developing creativity among children

1. INTRODUCTION

Dear Students, you know that thinking, problem; solving and creating some things which are novel to the person are some of the most complex activities of the human being. In the last chapter, we have discussed that intelligence of a person helps him to think rationally and to deal effectively with the environment. Individual differs from one another in their amount of intelligence. Here in this chapter you will know about creativity. You will also able to know like intelligence, creativity also differs from individual to individual. Creativity is a very important process for the progress and major advances in every field.

All the advances are made as a result of new ideas or creative process. It is the basis of the entire social development and new inventions and discoveries in the field or science and technology. Now, you may be very various to know more about creativity which is so important in our life. Let us discuss more details about it.

2. CONCEPT OF CREATIVIVY

Creativity was believed to be a gift of God long to be found in highly talented people and geniuses. Therefore, the view that the very intelligent or very superior people would be also creative was held. Creativity was regarded as a rare quality of distinguished individuals. A creative person has an inborn talent. The relationship between creativity and intelligence is neither linear nor curvilinear. For a longtime creativity was considered to be associated with artistic individuals who have been distinguished in various fields as painters, sculptures or writers. Creativity is distinguished by novelty, originality and is unusually inventive.

The more important feature of recent research is that creativity is not an extra ordinary gift, but a basic ability of all human beings. All persons to a certain degree potentially are creative. Helvetius (1758) was the first to recognize creativity not as a divine gift, but as a human quality. Contrary to the long held idea that it is a divine gift, it is now accepted that creativity exists in every sphere of human activity. People differ greatly on the degree creativity. The creative abilities may not have realized and remain potential owing to luck of proper stimulating conditions or owing to long neglect. So, I think all of you are now feeling very happy by knowing that you can also be a creative person by creating something new of your own ideas. Let us discuss how you can also create something.

Creativity is the power of the mind to form new ideas and thoughts. It helps you imagine something new and special. For example drawing, painting, writing, comes from being able to wonder, appreciate and think about things and be inspired by them. For example if you draw well and you see a beautiful painting, you begin to wonder at it's beauty. You ask yourself why you should not paint something as beautiful as the picture you have seen. Next day, you begin to draw or paint something of your own which is more beautiful than that you have seen. This is your creativity. So creativity brings out something special in you. Now, you must be clear about the concept of creativity. We will discuss some more examples of creativity for better clarity.

You know that many great poets have written poems on someone or something that made them wonder. Rudyard Kipling wondered about how a perfect man would be and wrote one of his most famous poem 'If'.

William Words Worth, on seeing a bed of daffodils was so wonderstruck by its beauty that the poem "daffodils" just flowed from his pen. Yet, the daffodil is one of the commonest blooms in England and millions just took them for granted and still do.

In the same way great painters made their most famous paintings. It is believed that Leonardo Davin a was inspired by a lady to paint the 'Monalisa'. You also know that Shahjahan's amazing Love for his wife Mumtaz Mahal, inspired the wonderous building the "Tajmahal".

Many very creative people wonder at even the tiniest, everyday aspects of life and then make their ideas into great works of painting, scripture and literature. You can also take up something you enjoy like drawing, music, dance etc. as you begin to enjoy if, you will become more and more creative in it. Even, ordinary, everyday things can be made into works of art like vegetable carving, dell making and matchbox building etc.

Some of the definitions given by different psychologists will also help us to get the meaning more clear.

1. Definitions of Creativity

"Creativity is the capacity of a person to produce compositions, products or ideas which are essentially new or novel and previously unknown to the producer."

- Drevdhal, J. E.

"Creative is a process extended in time and characterized by original adaptiveness and realization."

- Mc Kinnon

"A process is creative when it results in a novel work that is accepted as tenable, useful or satisfying by a group at a point in time."

- Taylor

"Creativity is a process sensing gaps or disturbing missing elements, forming ideas or hypotheses communicating the result, possibly modifying and re-testing hypotheses."

- Torrance

"It is distinguished between discovery, invention and creativity by saying that fact is discovered, theory is invented by only a masterpriece is created."

- Bronowsky

If we will analyse the definitions of creativity, it seems to fall under four categories.

- The person who Crates
- Mental processes asserting within the person who creates.
- Cultural and environmental factors working on the creator.
- Products of creativity, i.e. poems, paintings, theories and inventions.

Check Your Progress – I

Note: i) Write your answer in the space given.

ii) Check your answer.

i. Who recognize creative as a human quality?
ii. Who write the Poem Daffodils?
iii. Who painted the Monalisa?

3. NATURE AND CHARACTERISTICS OF CREATIVITY

All the definitions reveal the nature & characteristics of creativity.

- Creativity is the resultant of some interaction.
- Creativity is the ability to syntherise ideas or objects.
- It is a ability to create new ideas, theories or objects.
- It is a ability to develop something original.
- It is a process as well as a product.

- It is a complex & dynamic process.
- It knows no special medium, place, person or time.
- It is the capacity to accept challenge.
- It is readiness to change self and environment.

Though, creativity has some general characteristics, it's nature of work differs from person to person. For example creativity to the artist is the ability to evoke an emotional mood. To the architect, it is the ability to evolve new approaches, forms and new materials. To the Scientist, creativity is the ability to explore new way of extending knowledge. To the teacher, it is the ability to discover and apply dynamic methods of teaching learning whereas to the student it is the ability to use words and phrases in new situations, to solve sum speedily, to prepare new types of charts, to write essays and stories depicting new ideas.

Students, till now you learn about creativity, its concept, nature & characteristics. Now you will know the characteristics of a creative personality.

Torrance has compiled a list of eighty four characteristics of a creative person.

some of these are:-

- A creative person is very adventurous.
- He is flexible in his thinking, feeling & doing.
- He is very keen to explore and invent.
- He is intuitive, self-disciplined, visionary & willing to take risk.

On the whole, creative children are constantly probing, discovering, imaging, asking questions, guessing and wondering. Therefore, they should be encouraged to ask unusual questions, to explore new ways of thinking, to try novel approaches to problem solving, to play with ideas and material.

Check Your Progress – II

Note: Write your answer on the space given below

i. Write what according to you should be the main three characteristics of "Creativity".
ii. Write any four characteristics you observe in a creative person.

5. PROCESS OF CREATIVITY

The process of creative thinking involves some specific and definite steps these are:-

- Preparation
- Incubation
- Mumination or Inspiration and
- Verification or revision

Preparation:

Creative thinking in most fields of endeavored requires some preparation. It includes much trial and error. For example in writing a term paper, a student writes something, scratches out what he has written and starts over again, only to destroy that also. In this way continuous and persistent efforts are mode. At some point, he finds that he cannot solve the problem. So he keeps the work aside for the time being. Deliberately or involuntarily turning away from the problem is the beginning of the second stage which is known as incubation.

Incubation:

This stage is characterized by absence of activity or thinking about the problem. We can take rest or engage in other activities. Sometimes when we engaged in other work, this experience provides clue to the solution of the problem. For example Archimedes found the solution of the problem when he was taking his bath.

Illumination:

This experience of sudden appearance of the solution is known as inspiration or illumination. If occurs at any time, even in dreaming. A solution may appear when it is least expected. This process gives the insight or 'Aha' experience to the thinker. You know that how Archimedes came out of the bath-room by telling that "Eureka", "Eureka". This "Eureka" is the 'Aha' experience which is also known as illumination.

Verification:

During this stage illumination or inspiration is tried out. We determine whether the idea or solution appears suddenly is correct or not. In case if does not work well, fresh attempts are made for the solution. Sometimes the solution needs slight modification are change.

Then in the light of the results of verification or testing revision is made and the solution or idea is made workable. But at no stage, the creative thinkers thinks is made workable or idea is made workable. But at no stage, the creative thinkers think it completely project. It is open for essential modification or revision at any time when needed.

Though these are the difference stages in this process, skill you should not consider it as the rigid and fixed for all the times for all the thinkers because one may get the solution at the first stage, one may get the solution in the last stage, one may repeat the cycle again and again till for the a proper solution. However, these stages represent a scientific and systematic analysis of a higher creative process.

Check Your Process - III

Fill in the blanks.

i. The period when a person deliberately turning away from the problem is known as the period of ....
ii. In the process of creative thinking the 'Aha' experience comes in the stage.

6. MEASUREMENT OF CREATIVITY

You know that measurement is essential to know the existence of anything. So in case of creativity, we also need to measure creativity among individuals. According to Torrance, measurement of creativity is essential in identifying creative individuals. So, question may arise in your mind that why we should identify creative individuals? Identification of

creative individual is essential because it:-

- Enhances understanding of human mind and personality.
- Helps in individual teaching.
- Helps in guiding the mental growth and development.
- Emphasizes the need for guidance in future.
- Helps in arranging remedial programme.

Creativity can be identified in various areas like academic, artistic, mechanical and scientific etc. So, again a question may come to your mind that how creativity can be idealities in different areas? As every individual is unique, they also have their unique way of thinking. So they differ in their areas of interest. These areas can be identified by using various testing and non-testing techniques. These are:-

Observation: In this technique what you can to do is just to observe the behavior of the individual in different situations. From your observation you will be able to ideality the individual's creative areas.

Cumulative Record: If cumulative recorded is maintained about the individual, it also help you to know about the post activities of the individual. This record if property observed by you also enable you to identity the area of creativity of the same individual.

Informal Tests: You may ask small questions informally between the class discussions or general talks and may hope some idea about the individuals creative ability. For example you can ask questions like what changes will happen in our society after 10 years? How can you improve your mathematics laboratory? What will you do if you do not get sufficient food and money? Like this you can ask a number of questions from different areas to identity the creativity area.

Standardized Tests:

Different type of creativity tests developed by psychologists is used to measure creativity. Some of them are foreign tests and some are Indian tests.

Foreign tests:

Some standardized foreign tests used to measure creativity

are:-

- Guilford and Merifield test of creativity for college students.
- Burron and weish Art scale.
- Harris test of Scientific Creativity.

Indian Tests:

Like foreign tests, Indian tests are also developed to test the creativity in different areas. Some of these are:-

- Mazumdar Scientific Creativity Test
- ISPT Creativity Performance scale

- Chatteriee Mosaic Test
- Passi – A Battery of creativity Test

Besides these, Guilford and Merrifield have developed test techniques that measures fluency, flexibility, originality, re-definition and sensitivity to problems. Getzels and Jackson have used five different measures of Creativity in their research. They are:-

Word –Association – Tests : In this test students are required to give as many definitions and numbers of different categories into which they could be placed.

Uses of things tests: Here the students are asked to give as many uses as he can for a common object.

Hidden shapes Test: A student in this test is required to find more complex form of figure on card in a simple form.

Three difference Endings: A student is required to suggest three different endings to an incomplete short tables.

Make up problems: A student is required to makeup as many mathematical problems he can on the basis of information given in a complex paragraph.

There are also minessola tests of creative thinking comprising non-verbal tests like picture construction, creative design, circles, and shares, etc. you can also refer to Torrance's checklist comprising eighty-four characteristics for identifying the creative children.

Check Your Progress – IV

Note: Write the answers in the space given below.

i. Prepare a creativity test using the five measures given by Getzels & Jackson.

7. USES OF CREATIVITY TEST

If anything you will prepare, you must think how this can be used. Here you know that how creativity can be idealities & you also have prepared a creativity test. So you should use it. Before using it, you should know how you can use it.

You know that creativity is a natural endowment. If needs stimulation and nourishment. Most of creative talent if not given proper training, education and opportunity for creativity expression, results in wastage.

Moreover, creativity is universal. It is not monopoly of a few geniuses only. Every one of us to certain degree possesses creative abilities. In a democratic set up like owners, it is not only the geniuses who are needed to create, manifest and produce, others whether mediocre or below averages are also required to think construct and creatively.

Creativity tests are useful in finding the nature and amount of creativity among the children. This also helps us to provide proper environment and guidance to develop the originality of the individual in a full-fledged way. We can organize various activities and situations to develop creativity among children according to their abilities. These are:-

Freedom to Respond:

Adequate freedom should be given to children in responding to a situation. They should be encouraged to think about as many ideas as they may for the solution of the problem.

Opportunity for involvement:

The feelings like "It is my creation", "I have solved" give much satisfaction to children. Therefore opportunity should be provided to them to derive satisfaction from being a cause.

Encouraging originality and flexibility:

Originality on the part of children in any form should be encouraged. They should also be asked problem questions to answer. In learning a task if they need to change their methods of learning, hey should essentially be encouraged to do it.

Removal of heritation and fear:

The cause of haritation and fear for doing any work should be discovered and removed as far as possible.

Providing appropriate opportunities and atmosphere:

A healthy favorable atmosphere for creative thinking and expression is an essential condition for the stimulation and nourishment of creativity among children.

Developing healthy habits among children:

Industriousness, persistence, reliance and self-confidence are some of the qualities that are helpful in creative output.

Therefore children should be helped to imbibe these qualities.

Using the Creative resources of the Community:

Children should be made to visit the centers of creative art or scientific and industrial creative work. Occasionally, the creative artists, scientists or creative persons from other fields may also invited which will be helpful in enhancing the span of knowledge of children and kindly the spark of creativity among them.

Avoidance of Blocks to Creative thinking:

Factors like conservatism, faculty methods of teaching, rigid habits of work, un sympathetic treatment should be avoided.

Proper organization of the curriculum:

Curriculum should reflect what if desires from the creative children in terms of fluency, flexibility, originality, divergent thinking, inventiveness and elaboration etc.

Use of Special Techniques:

Besides these uses, special techniques also should be used to foster creativity, Researchers have suggested some special techniques like.

Brain Storming:

It is a technique which emphasizes the important of divergent thinking. It involves generating ideas in response some problem in a group. It allows children to attack and solve a problem without any inhibition or restriction.

Providing the self-examples and ideals

"Self-example is better than precept.' Children are very imitative. Therefore the presents, teachers and elders should try to develop the habit of creative thinking among them.

Besides these, gaming techniques, showing with and humane, encouraging debates, discussions, quick and providing activities like drama, dance music etc. should be arranged for the children to develop their creativity.

After identifying creative children adequate and appropriate provisions should be made for their education and training, because the future of mankind depends upon the development of their creative potential.

Check your Progress- V

i. Write two ways of Brain storming.
ii. Write what according to you are the two best ways of using creative resources of the community.

8. LET US SUM UP

In this unit we have discussed that creativity is necessary for problem solving. But are all problems demands creative solutions? No. For example there is only one correct answer to the question a how much is 75 plus 25? But an architect asked design a new museum for a particular community might produce a variety of design solutions. When asked to solve a problem or form a concept, people may respond without much though in a pre-determined manner, or they form a hypothesis and then test it to evaluate potential solutions. For particularly difficult problem, a creative solution is often best, although it may not be an obvious one. A creative solution is one that makes others say 'why did not I think of that? It is not always easy to define a creative solution. Similarly, it is not always easy to identify a creative individual.

This unit gives you idea creativity is the process of developing original, novel and yet appropriate response to a problem. A novel response is one that is new or that has no precedent. An original response is one that is not usually given. However, unless an original and novel solution is also appropriate, it cannot be termed creative, though not too easy, still by observing carefully the characteristics of a creative person and administering different creativity tests, a creative person can be identified by you. On that basis you can create situations, provide facilities to develop creativity among them. Sometimes creative individuals experience a sudden brilliant illumination,

but more often their new ideas come about through a slow intuitive understanding of the field of endeavor. Their back-ground allows them to be constructively creative. This unit is an attempt to give an outline of how the nature and characteristics of creativity & creative individuals help in identifying creative individuals. Different types of creativity tests & their uses in educational situation are also part of this unit. In short, this unit gives an awareness to the parents, teachers and elders about their role in promoting creativity among children.

Unit End Exercises

1. i) Helvitius

ii. William words worth

iii. Leonardo Da Vinci

2. i) Novelty, originality & appropriateness

ii) Curiosity, imagining, adventurous & asking questions

3. i) Incubation

ii) Illumination/ Imspiration

4. Word association Test –

Uses of thing Tests – Ten uses of 'Scale'

Hidden shape Test – Providing card or paper of different size & asking to prepare as many pictures can be drawn using it.

Three different endings – Write an incomplete story asking to complete the story in three different way.

Make-up Problems – Give a paragraph of information & ask the students to prepare many problems on the basis of the information.

5. i) 'Organising a function' & "Student self government in schools"

ii) Visit to centres of creative work and inviting creative persons from other fields for leature.

Exercises

1. What is creativity? Explain its nature & characteristics.
2. Who is a creative child? What are his chief characteristics?
3. Define creativity. Explain how can you identify creativity among children.
4. Explain the role of parents and teachers in the promotion of creativity in children.
5. Write short note on the following questions within 150 words.

a. Steps in creative process
b. Uses of creativity
c. Brain storming
d. Creativity Tests

????

CHAPTER-12

GROUP DYNAMICS

Unit structure:

0. Objectives

1. Introduction
2. Group Dynamics

   1. Meaning
   2. Process of Group Dynamics
   3. Importance of Group Dynamics

3. Group Mind

   1. Meaning
   2. Importance of Group Mind.

4. Techniques of Group Learning

   1. Co - operative Learning
   2. Group Discussion

5. Let us sum up
6. Glossary
7. Suggested reading

0. OBJECTIVES

- To develop an understanding of group dynamics.
- To develop an understanding of the process of group dynamics.
- To gain insight into the importance of group dynamics and group mind.
- To acquaint the learners with the different techniques of group learning.

1. INTRODUCTION

Introduction to Group Dynamics

Human beings exhibit some characteristic behavior patterns when interacting in groups. Therefore, understanding group behavior plays a vital role in order to establish a harmonious society.

The psychology of the group is also called group behavior. The group helps a person in the satisfaction of his fundamental needs and in achieving a sense of accomplishment. In modern organizations, groups are employed as major instruments for operations, particularly for problem- solving and improving performance.

Meaning of a Group:-

It has been commonly observed and also established through various experimental studies that there are differences in the behavior of an individual when they are alone and when they are together in a group. As a member of a group, he exhibits group behavior. When two or more people come together it is known as a Group. A group is one in which people come together to attain a common goal & the relations among the members are interdependent i.e. each members behavior influences the behavior of the others in the group.

According to Mill, "A unit composed of two or more persons who come together to achieve a specific purpose & consider a contact meaningful is a GROUP."

Bass approached the definition of a group in the angle of motivation & satisfaction of needs.

Bogurdas defines a group as, "A collection of two or more persons with common interest, stimulating each other having common loyalty & participating in common activities."

Characteristics of a Group:A typical group must have the following essential characteristics in order to be called a group in the psychological sense.

1. **Leadership:** - According to Carter, a leader is a person who is able to lead the group towards the attainment of the goal. The teacher helps the students in the attainment of the goals. In that sense, the teacher is the leader of the classroom group.

2. **Interdependency/ Common Interest:** - The members of a group have common and well defined goals, interest and ideals. Every member tries to attain the goals set down by the society

e.g. members of rotary club have a common aim of social work for the benefit of underprivileged. The behavior of one member of a group influences that of the other and in this way his own behavior is influenced. This type of relationship is also known as psychological relationship.

3. **Cohesiveness (Oneness):** - There is a sense of oneness in the group because of the similarity in interest. A member looks upon other as related to him. In this way, good feelings, devotion, faithfulness, adjustment, suggestion & imitation are developed amongst the members.

4. **Conformity (Comply by the rules set within the group):** - The members of the group have to adhere to the rules set by the group. The actions of members are controlled by the group. All the members of the group follow the ideals & traditions of the group.

5. **Organized structure:** - Any group has an organized structure which is well defined .e.g. The class is an organized structure which is homogeneous with respect to age, subject, etc.

6. **Motivation/ Mutual Obligation:** - The degree of motivation or the motivational level that exists among the members of the group should be the same. It is such a power as keeps not only the members of the group united but also provides them with energy e.g. the relationship between the children & parents in the family or the love of husband & wife. In spite of differences, they have certain common aims, ideals & values. We-feeling is developed leading to the development of affinity in the group. Social values are also developed.

2. GROUP DYNAMIC

1. Meaning of Group Dynamics:

It is a relatively new concept in the socio – psychological field. Etymologically, the word, Dynamic, is derived from a Greek word, which means 'force'. Thus, Group Dynamics stands for the forces operating in a group. A group is constantly interacting, thereby bringing about a perpetual change in the personality and behavior of the members constituting the group. The behavior is not static. Group Dynamics means the change of behavior through interaction in the group. It refers to the forces which operate in group situations. It studies the structure of the group and other phenomenon which emerge out of group interaction.

- According to the Goods dictionary – "Group Dynamics implies an interactive psychological relationship in which members of a group develop a common perception based on feelings and emotions. These inter-stimulative relationships may be described by the term Group Dynamics."

- Kretch & Crutch - Group Dynamics implies changes that take place within groups.
- Thus group dynamics is the study of forces exerted by the group on the individual or the individual on the group.

2. Process of Group Dynamics: -

- Argyle (1969) categorized 4 stages in the "life" of a group
    - forming
    - storming
    - norming
    - performing
- Heron (1989) identified a fifth stage
    - Mourning / Adjourning

- **Forming** - This is when a group first gets together. People tend to find out about each other, consider purposes, brainstorm ideas and possible structures for tasks and consider their own roles within the group. This is usually a very sociable time in the life of the group.
- **Storming** - As the group begins to settle in and individuals get to know each other, they may start competing for status and role in the group. Disagreements occur and where some members may try to assert strong opinions or leadership tactics, others may withdraw. If tensions are not mutually dealt with at this stage, they tend to disrupt group communication and activity, and most importantly, mutual respect for the roles of members. To reach stages (c) and (d) conflicts need to be resolved.
- **Norming** - After the more tense stage of storming, the group usually begins to settle as members have found a common approach to the task that all agree upon or accept (this is where unsettled conflicts can be problematic as they will probably reoccur later). Action plans begin to emerge and people find space to begin working on tasks.
- **Performing** - This is the stage when the group achieves optimum efficiency and work gets done. At this stage it is important to know the team work strategies you are working with (Sharples, 1999: 71) that will best utilize the expertise of each member. It is also useful be aware of time spent on each task through a log or diary, so that possible conflicts do not reoccur.
- **Mourning / Adjourning** - Having satisfactorily got through the group tasks, if the group has been successful in working together, despite initial tensions and conflicts, we often see members sad to leave each other. This is where mutual respect and achievement is felt most significantly. Often sub-groups form from the larger groups to continue with personal or professional development interests.

3. Importance of developing Group Dynamics in Learning:

1. **To improve the behavior of students** - In a class room group, the students come into contact with each other and acquire appropriate type of education.

2. **To develop mental processes** - Some sort of exchange of thoughts goes on in the class group through which intellectual activities like reasoning, memory, judgments, decisions, thinking and imagination develop.

3. **To develop the feeling of self sacrifice** - The students in a class room group remain in close contact with each other. Therefore so much love, good will and sympathy develops in them that in the time of need they do not hesitate to sacrifice themselves for the sake of others.

4. **To prepare for future social life** - Children in class room group live together for pretty long time and try to adjust their thoughts, habits and viewpoints to others. Such a type of experience prepares them for future social life.

5. **To excite sympathy of numbers** - A student starts doing as other students do. Their tendency is called sympathy of numbers.

6. **To develop qualities of leadership** - Students in classroom groups plan or organize a number of co-curricular activities. Thus qualities of leadership are developed in them.

7. **To acquire more knowledge** - In a classroom group the students learn the habits of competition and imitation and get an inspiration to acquire more knowledge.

8. **To develop the feeling of co-operation** - The teacher encourages all the members of a classroom group to work together and thus feeling of cooperation is developed in them.

Check your progress

1. What is a group? What are the basic characteristics of a group?
2. What is group Dynamics? Why is it important for a teacher to know about the dynamics of a group?

3. GROUP MIND

1. Group Mind

Sociologist, Lebon has used this term for explaining the various characteristics of crowd behavior. Lebon asserted that individuals behave in a peculiar way when there are members of crowd. Explaining the reasons for this, Lebon says that individuals as a member of crowd are in the grip of collective or group mind and thus behave differently. At this time, as a member of crowd their unconscious personality disappears and it is their conscious personality moved by the group mind that is responsible for their peculiar behavior.

Various sociologist and psychologist like Mc Dougall use this term as a concept to explain the behavior of individuals as members of highly stable enduring groups like the army or some political and religious organizations. He asserted that members of these highly organized well-integrated groups behave differently in these groups as they would otherwise behave as an individual outside these groups.

Thus, the concept of group mind has been made into use for explaining our peculiar behavior as a member of crowd or a highly organized and integrated group.

2. Importance of Group Mind:

School is a social group. All the students and teachers are its members. A School has a purpose of imparting education .The atmosphere of school persuades new members to join the group and continues making efforts to modify the behavior of elder members. Several types of conditions are essential for building up an organized school community. They are as under:

1. **Continuous existence of the community** - The school community is not like a crowd. It has stability. Teachers remain in the school for long time. A large number of students study in the school and in this way it is stable. For its stability, it is essential that the teachers do not change often and students do not leave it after studying for sometimes. They stay at school for considerable time so that they may understand the value of school society and acquire its good virtues.

2. **Aims of a school** - All schools have aims and ideals to be realized. They have their own traditions which help in molding the personality of the child as per the requirements of the society. There is a close affinity developed towards their institution by participating in various activities. The schools should organize activities like annual day, sports day, exhibitions, morning assembly etc. so that there is a lot of

interaction among students and with teachers which helps in developing a we feeling, thereby instilling pride towards their alma mater.

3. **Social feelings and pride in traditions** - The young students of a school feel proud of their school. The students of different schools compare the activities of their schools and each student tries to prove that his school is the better one. Individuals compete in debates, sports, games, one act play etc. and develop in the students for the school. Tradition of the school, results, sports, cultural activities etc produces a feeling of rivalry among the students. Students are ready to do many a thing to bring self-respect & glory to their alma mater. All these things help in developments of social feelings in them.

4. **Co-operative and creative atmosphere** - The school is an organized group. It is essential that the students work in co-operation with each other. In order to achieve this, the teacher will have to lead them. As far as possible, individual competition should not be encouraged but group game should be organized E.g. inter-class game competitions, etc.

It is essential for the school environment to be creative and progressive. It should change with time so that it remains the mirror of the school. Its aim should be decided. It should lead the society. Such a thing is possible only in the creative atmosphere of the school.

Check your progress

1. Explain the process of group formation/ life stages of a group?
2. What is group mind? How does the knowledge of group mind help a teacher?

4. TECHNIQUES OF GROUP LEARNING

1. Techniques of Group Learning - Co-operative Learning **Cooperative learning** is the instructional use of small groups so that students work together to maximize their own as well as each other's learning. Class members are organized into small groups after receiving instruction from the teacher. They then work through

the assignment until all group members successfully understand and complete it. Cooperative efforts result in participants striving for mutual benefit so that all group members gain from each other's efforts.

Some Basic Cooperative Learning Strategies:-

1. Three-Step Interview:

Form pairs of students. The teacher may ask students to read necessary matter beforehand.

Step One: One student interviews another within specified time limits. e.g. In order to study the topic 'Learning', the following questions may be asked: What is meant by learning? When does learning occur? Give an example of when learning does not occur.

Step Two: The two then reverse roles and conduct the interview again. Same questions or similar type of questions may be used

Step Three: In a learning team composed of two pairs, the students then share the highlights of the information or insights got from the paired interview.

2. Roundtable:

Roundtable, a cooperative learning structure useful for brainstorming, reviewing, or practicing a skill, uses a single sheet of paper and pen for each cooperative learning group. Students in the group respond in turn to a question or problem by stating their ideas aloud as they write them on the paper. Team members are encouraged not to skip turns, but if their thoughts are at a standstill, they are allowed to say "Pass" rather than to turn the brainstorm into a brain drizzle. Thus, there is almost universal participation in Roundtable. Students, for example, could identify the characteristics of an effective leader or the attributes of terrorism before these topics are formally introduced. Comparing a student- generated list with those of the "experts," creates interest. In Roundtable, the multiple answers encourage creativity and deeper thinking.

3. Think-Pair-Share:

Think: In this activity the instructor poses a question, preferably one demanding analysis, evaluation, or synthesis, and gives **students** thirty seconds or more to think through an appropriate response. This time can also be spent writing the response.

Pair: After this "wait time," students then turn to partners and share their responses.

Share: During the third and last stage, student responses can be shared within learning teams, with larger groups, or with the entire class during a follow-up discussion.

4. Gallery Walk:

Assign a topic to be studied by a group. Let the group depict their thoughts, understanding of the topic by means of a concept map. All groups put up their products for the rest of the groups to see. One spokesperson remains near the group's chart while the other members take a gallery walk to see what others have done. Queries will be answered by the spokesperson. The spokesperson role should be rotated so that no one is left without the stimulation of exploring the different student creations.

5. Jigsaw:

The students in a history class, for example, are divided into small groups of five or six students each. Suppose their task is to learn about World War II. In one jigsaw group, Sara is responsible for researching Hitler's rise to power in pre-war Germany. Another member of the group, Steven, is assigned to cover concentration camps; Pradeep is assigned Britain's role in the war; Meeta is to research the contribution of the Soviet Union; Tahira will handle Japan's entry into the war; Rachna will read about the development of the atom bomb. Eventually each student will come back to her or his jigsaw group and will try to present a well-organized report to the group. The situation is specifically structured so that the only access any member has to the other five assignments is by listening closely to the report of the person reciting.

6. Circle the Sage:

Divide the class into teams of say 4 to 5 members. Select some students from the class who will be able to explain a concept to the students. Those students (the sages) stand and spread out in the room. The teacher then has the rest of the classmates each surround a sage, with no two members of the same team going to the same sage. The sage explains what they know while the classmates listen, ask questions, and take notes. All students then return to their teams. Each in turn, explains what they learned. Because each one has gone to a different sage, they compare notes. If there is disagreement, they stand up as a team. Finally, the disagreements are aired and resolved.

2. <u>Techniques of Group Learning – Group Discussions</u>

A Group Discussion is a methodology frequently used by an organization to gauge whether the candidate has certain personality traits and/or skills that it desires in its members. In this methodology, the group of candidates is given a topic or a situation, given a few minutes to think about the same, and then asked to discuss it among themselves for 15-20 minutes. How a particular candidate handles, the topic, the interruptions, etc. brings to fore his clarity of concepts, his ability to express himself and his handling of social behavioral patterns.

Some of the personality traits that one can gauge through a Group Discussion are:

- Ability to work in a team
- Communication skills
- Reasoning ability
- Leadership skills
- Initiative
- Assertiveness
- Flexibility
- Creativity
- Ability to think on ones feet

The aspects which make up a Group Discussion are verbal communication, non-verbal behavior, conformation to norms, decision-making ability and cooperation.

A school, too, is a social organization and the technique of Group Discussion can be used by a teacher to clarify concepts and also to impart essential social skills. Such discussions can be held in the classroom itself and topics from the subject, itself can be used. This method of learning helps in enhancing a student's communication skills and other skills for personality development such as it checks

- how one behaves, participates and contributes in a group,
- how much importance does a child give to the group objective as well as his own,
- how well do one listens to viewpoints of others and how open-minded one is in accepting views contrary to one's own.

5. LET US SUM UP:

- When two or more people come together it is known as a Group. A group is one in which people come together to attain a common goal & the relations among the members are interdependent. Thus, a unit composed of two or more persons who come together to achieve a specific purpose & consider a contact meaningful is a GROUP.
- A group is characterized by Leadership, Interdependency, Cohesion, Conformity, Organized structure and Motivation.
- Group Dynamics means the change of behavior through interaction in the group. It refers to the forces which operate in group situations. It studies the structure of the group and other phenomenon which emerge out of group interaction.
- The five stages in the life of a group are: Forming, Storming, Norming Performing and Mourning.
- Individuals behave in a peculiar way when there are members of crowd as they are in the grip of collective or group mind. As a member of a crowd, their unconscious personality disappears and it is their conscious personality moved by the group mind that is responsible for their peculiar behavior.
- Co-operative learning as well as Group Discussions are some of the techniques of Group Learning.
- Cooperative learning is the instructional use of small groups so that students work together to maximize their own as well as each other's learning
- A Group Discussion is a methodology used to gauge whether an individual has certain personality traits and/or skills that a group desires in its members.

Check your progress...

1. How can a teacher use the technique of cooperative learning to enhance her student's learning? Illustrate.
2. Group Discussions helps in developing learning and social skills in an individual. Discuss.

6. GLOSSARY

Group: A collection of two or more persons with common interest, stimulating each other having common loyalty & participating in common activities.

Group Dynamics: the study of forces exerted by the group on the individual or the individual on the group.

Group Mind: the peculiar behavior of an individual as a member of crowd or a highly organized and integrated group.

Co-operative Learning: the instructional use of small groups so that students work together to maximize their own as well as each other's learning.

Group Discussion: a methodology used to gauge whether an individual has certain personality traits and/or skills that a group desires in its members.

????

References:

Aggarwal J. C. (2004) Psychology of learning & development, Shipra Publishers, N. Delhi

Aggarwal J. C. 92001) Basic ideas in Educational Psychology, Shipra Publisher, N. Delhi

Aggrawal J. C. (1995) Essentials of Educational Psychology, Vikas Publ House, N. Delhi

Bhatia KK (1989) Educational Psychology & Techniques of teaching, N. Delhi

Bhatia HR (1986) Elements of Educational Psychology, Bombay Bhatia HR (1997) A text book of Educational Psychology, N. Delhi

Bhatnager Suresh & Saxena Anamika (2007) Advanced Educational Psychology, R Lall Book Depot, Meerut

Bhatnager R, P. Educational Psychology, Meenakshi Publications, Kanpur

Bhattacharya Srinibas (2002): Psychological Foundations of Education, Atlantic Publishers, N. Delhi

Cascio, Wayne F. & Agunis Herman- Applied Psychology in Human Resource Management, Prentice Hall of India, N. Delhi

Chauhan SS (1990) Advanced Educational Psychology, Vikas Publication House, N. Delhi

Chatterjee SK: Advanced Educational Psychology Crow LD & Crow A- Educational Psychology

S. A. Texbook of Advanced Education Psychology

Dandekar & Makhija (1988) – Psychological foundations of Education, Madras

Dandekar WN (1975): Fundamentals of Experimental Psychology, Poona.

Hergenhahn BR & Olson Matthew H: An introduction to Theories of Learning, Prentice Hall of India, N. Delhi

Kakkar SB (1989): Education Psychology & Guidance, Ambala

Lahey RB. Graham JE & others: An Introduction to Educational Psychology, 6th edition, Tata McGraw Hill Publ,

Lefrancois Guy, R: Theories of Human learning

Mangal SK: Educational Psychology, Prentice Hall of India, N. Delhi

Mangal SK: Essentials of Educational Psychology, Prentice Hall of India, N. Delhi

Mathur SS (1983): Educational Psychology, Agra Mathur SS; Advanced Educational Psychology

Rajamanickam M. Experimental Psychology with Advanced Experiments, Vol 1& 2, Concept Publishing Co, N. Delhi

Sharma, Y. P., & veer Singh, A. (2015), The Role of Emotional Attachment of Teachers in the Development of Self-confidence, Learning Habits and Social Adjustment of Children in the Primary Schools

Sharma, D. Y. P. (2020), SPECIAL EDUCATION: EDUCATION OF CHILDREN WITH SPECIAL NEEDS, Paperback & E-Book with ISBN-13: 978-1658036535 on January 10, 2020, by Kindle Direct Publishing

Sharma, D.Y. P. (2020), GUIDANCE AND COUNSELLING, Paperback & E-Book with ISBN-13: 979-8646052132 on May 19, 2020, by Kindle Direct Publishing

Sharma, D.Y. P. (2020), "Philosophy of Education" Paperback& E-Book with ISBN-13:978-620-2-79835-8on September 17, 2020, by LAP LAMBERT Academic Publishing Germany

Sharma RA (1996) Essentials of Educational Psychology, R Lall Book Depot, Meerut

Sharma RN & Sharma RK (2002) Educational Psychology, Atlantic Publishers & Distributors, N. Delhi.

Sharma RN & Sharma RK (2003) Advance Educational Psychology, Atlantic Publishers & Distributors, N. Delhi

Tara Chand (1993) Educational Psychology N Delhi Walia JS: Foundational of Educational Psychology

Woolfolk AR (1995) Educational Psychology, 6th edition, Allyn & Bacon, Boston.

www.google.com

https://archive.mu.ac.in/myweb_test/SYBA%20Study%20Material/edu-II%20psycho.pdf

enwikipediaorg/wiki/Psychologyoflearning

????

Contents

9 798885 692618

Printed by Libri Plureos GmbH in Hamburg,
Germany